GOD'S ENCOURAGING
PRESENCE

BY
CAROL S. LEWIS

PRESS

Marilyn,

Be Blessed With
God's Love And
Presence.

Love,
Carol A Lewis
Galatians 2:20

To: Marilyn
From: Love, Rita
Christmas 2015

PREFACE

"God's Encouraging Presence" was birthed over three decades of messages given to me during a time of prayer. It is a collection of personal words to the reader with the intent of comforting, strengthening and encouraging the believer in Christ. (I Corinthians 14:3)

Each message has a key word addressing a particular need. The whole message, or just a portion of it, can minister to you depending on the Holy Spirit's application to your life. They are to be conformational to the way the Lord Jesus has already been working in you. (Philippians 1:6)

It is my prayer that as you read these, you will sense a greater desire to follow Jesus more, to get into His Word and study it, and be encouraged in your faith that no matter what you are facing, God has an encouraging word for you to hear.

May the God who gives endurance and encouragement give you a spirit of unity among yourselves as you follow Christ Jesus, so that with one heart and mouth you may glorify the God and Father of our Lord Jesus Christ. -Romans 15:5-6, 9 (NIV)

CSL

DEDICATION

For my children David, Kimberly and Nancy

For my grandchildren Parker, Mason, Bennett, Zander, Joseph,
Daniel, Renee Gabriella, Timothy, Nicholas,
Ashley, Samantha

And for my future grandchildren

Let this be written for a future generation,
that a people not yet created may praise the Lord.
Psalm 102:18 (NIV)

ACKNOWLEDGMENTS

T hanking God for the many friends who encouraged me to put these messages in book form.

For Jackie Stein and Rita Caponi who prayed me through each step of the process.

For Kendra Jones who tirelessly worked to get the manuscript ready for publication.

For my brother, Gary Roy Andersen, who took the cover picture of my Father's hands, Lars Roy Andersen.

Most of all for my Lord and Savior, Jesus Christ, who gets all the Glory for this book.

TABLE OF CONTENTS

I, TO MY SONS AND DAUGHTERS 15

Are You Fully Surrendered ....Abandonment
Does Your Marriage Need Deliverance .... Adultery
Do you Need Healing ....Affliction
Is God Calling You To Teach.........................Authority
Have You Been Away From God .... Backslidden
Are You Sent Out Together .... Blending
Is Satan Trying To Keep You From Church ....Buffeting
Is This A Special Day................................Comfort
Is God Asking You To Trust Your Husband .... Confidence
Do You Need Direction ....Confirmation
Do You Have A Mother's Heart .... Consoling
Do You Need Encouragement........................Courage
Do You Need Creative Ideas .... Creativity
Are You Coming To A Cross Road .... Decisions
Have You Failed.......................................Defeat
Are You In Depression............................. Depression
Are You Confused ....Direction
Is God Training You................................ Discipline
Has God Expanded Your Ministry ....Expansion
Are You Worried About Your Daughter ....Expectations
Are You Contemplating Building ....Exploits
Are You Looking For Your Family To Be Used ....Family

Do You Need Forgiveness . . . . .Forgiveness

Do You Need A Breakthrough . . . . Freedom

Are You Too Old For God To Use . . . . .Fruitfulness

Are Your Desires Fulfilled . . . . Fulfillment

Is God Using The Two Of You . . . . God's Voice

Do You Believe Your Ministry Is Over . . . . .Going Forward

Are You Afraid To Trust God . . . . Growing Up

Does Your Ministry Need Growth. Growth

Are You Seeking Anointed Guidance . . . . .Guidance

Do You Believe Satan Or God. . . . . Guilt Free

Is Your Husband Discouraged . . . . Hope

Daughter, Is God Calling You To Minister Encouragement Inspiration

Are You Led To Pray For The Nation . . . . .Intercession

Is The Holy Spirit Calling You . . . . .Invitation

Do You Want Revelation Knowledge . . . . Kingdom Secrets

Are You Waiting For Marching Orders . . . . Leadership/Women

Are You Holding On To The Past .Letting Go

Are You In Fear Of Dying . . . . Life

Are You In Trouble. . . . . .New Beginnings

Are You Ready To Evangelize . . . . .Obedience

Do You Communicate With Your Wife. . . . . .Oneness

Are You Waiting On God . . . . .Patience

Are You Struggling With Sin . . . . .Perseverance

Is God Giving You His Building Blueprint. . . . . Plans

Does The Land Belong To You . . . . .Possession

Are You An Intercessor . . . . Prayer

Son-Is God Preparing You. . . . . Preparation

Is God's Word Important To You. . . . . Priorities

Is All Lost . . . . Promises

Are You Called To Speak To Crowds . . . . .Promotion

Does Your Ministry Need Money .Provisions

Do You Feel Unqualified To Lead. . . . . Qualifications

Are You Reaching Out To Your Brothers . . . . Reaching Out

Are You Pulling Back. . . . . .Resistance

Are You Asked To Call The Praying Women . . . . .Response

Have You Been Sacrificially Praising Me . . . . Sacrifice
Do You Want To Know God Better . . . . Seeking
Have You Trouble Speaking . . . . Speaking
Are You In Pain . . . . Suffering
Have You Been A Faithful Writer . . . . .Talents
Do You Have Trouble Controlling Your Tongue . . . . Temperance
Are You A Man Called Of God .Tender Shoot
Are You Timid . . . . .Timidity
Are You Bearing A Special Burden . . . . .Training
Mother, Are You In Travail . . . . Travailing
Has Your Husband Hurt You . . . . Trust
Do You Feel God Has Forgotten You . . . . .Understanding
Do You Want To Sing . . . . .Unhindered
Do You Need Unity With Your Spouse . . . . Unity
Are You In The Holy of Holies . . . . .Victory
Is Satan Buffeting Your Healing Ministry . . . . Warfare
Are You Praying The Word . . . . Weapons
Do You Want Tomorrow To Be Special . . . . .Worship
Are You Like Timothy . . . . Youthful

II.TO MY SHEPHERDS 137

Is God Calling Your Congregation To Prayer . . . . Assembly
Have Your Funds And Home Been Stolen . . . . .Blessings
Is Your Church In Division . . . . .Divisions
Is Your Church Called To Evangelize . . . . .Evangelism
Is Your Flock Young . . . . Example
Have You Been Waiting For God's Blessing . . . . .Faithfulness
Have You Been Wrongly Accused . . . . .False Accusation
Do You Need Greater Love . . . . Love
Do They Still Want Milk . . . . Maturity
Is Your Ministry Small . . . . Numbers
Are There Obstacles In Your Church . . . . .Obstacles
Are You Above Your Congregation . . . . Servant Hood
Is God Speaking Concerning Healing . . . . .Spiritual Gifts
Do You Desire The Holy Spirit Upon Your Flock . . . Spiritual Hunger

Is God Moving Too Slow For You . . . . .Timing
Is God Calling The Elders Together . . . . Vision

<u>III.TO MY CHURCH 169</u>

To The Church of California
To The Church of Illinois
To The Church of Maine, Connecticut & New Hampshire
To The Church of New York
To The Church of The West
To The Church of Washington D.C.
I Will Chasten. . . . . .Chasten
I Seek Childlikeness. . . . . .Childlike
Is Your Body Holy . . . . Holiness
Your Praise Delights Me . . . . .Praise
I Will Vindicate My Body . . . . Vindication
Work While It Is Day . . . . Work

I. TO MY SONS AND DAUGHTERS

If I speak in the tongues of men and of angels, but have not love, I am only a resounding gong or a clanging cymbal. If I have the gift of prophecy and can fathom all mysteries and all knowledge, and if I have a faith that can move mountains, but have not love, I am nothing. If I give all I possess to the poor and surrender my body to the flames, but have not love, I gain nothing.

Love is patient, love is kind. It does not envy, it does not boast, it is not proud. It is not rude, it is not self-seeking, it is not easily angered, it keeps no record of wrongs. Love does not delight in evil but rejoices with the truth. It always protects, always trusts, always hopes, always perseveres.

Love never fails. But where there are prophecies, they will cease; where there are tongues, they will be stilled; where there is knowledge, it will pass away. For we know in part and we prophesy in part, but when perfection comes, the imperfect disappears.

When I was a child, I talked like a child, I thought like a child, I reasoned like a child. When I became a man, I put childish ways behind me. Now we see but a poor reflection as in a mirror; then we shall see face to face. Now I know in part; then I shall know fully even as I am fully known.

And now these three remain: faith, hope and love. But the greatest of these is love.- I Corinthians 13 (NIV)

ARE YOU FULLY SURRENDERED

My ways are always of hope, deliverance, healing, prosperity and life. In me dwells the fullness of the Godhead. I am looking today for men, women, and children who will be sold out to me in all things. I am looking for people who will not be concerned about the ways of the world, but in me and me alone. I am looking for vessels of purity, righteousness and holiness. My Spirit is moving swiftly upon the face of the earth to draw all men unto me.

My Spirit is moving swiftly to bring my body into unity. My Spirit is moving swiftly to elevate my children to places of leadership. My Spirit is moving swiftly to open the prison doors of those bound in captivity in other parts of the world.

Pestilence may come. Famine may abound. Destruction may be everywhere, but where My Spirit is moving in the life of my child, it does not touch him. Suffering for my Kingdom and my Kingdom alone must come. But know this my child, that wherever my name is breathed, there is hope, deliverance and life.

I love you my children. I have so much stored up for you. Be faithful to me and blessings, even in a crisis, will abound, joy in spite of sorrow released, life in place of death felt. My Spirit is holy and in his holiness, sin cannot dwell.

Love me with all of your heart, soul and mind. I loved you before you even knew me. I loved you and called you to be my very own. I gave you an inheritance with the living so what is life can swallow what is death. Give me your body, your tongue and your very all. Let my Spirit cleanse out what is not of me. I have blessings to give all of my children, blessings that are just for the asking.

Pray and worship me. Praise me, praise me, praise me in all things and life in its fullness will abound, in spite of what seems like destruction. Give to me glory, glory, glory, from lips of adoration, love and devotion.

I am doing a new thing throughout the world. My angels are ministering, my hosts ministering, my body ministering. My return is soon. The days will come when the winds of my Spirit will cease. I look forward to seeing all of you face to face. Hold on! Hold on! Hold on! Be faithful. I love you! I love you! I love you!

Therefore. I urge you, brothers, in view of God's mercy, to offer your bodies as living sacrifices, holy and pleasing to God—this is your spiritual act of worship. Do not conform any longer to the pattern of this world, but be transformed by the renewing of your mind. Then you will be able to test and approve what God's will is—his good, pleasing and perfect will. Romans 12:1-2

ABANDONMENT

DOES YOUR MARRIAGE NEED DELIVERANCE

Y ou have been fighting Satan's hosts since the conception of your marriage. Yes, you have been fighting the hosts of hell. You have been fighting an unseen army, unequipped and not knowing my real power. But, within both of you lies a reservoir, an untapped resource of might and strength, a gold mine of power to fight off the attacks of the enemy.

Satan does prowl like a roaring lion. He seeks to devour you both. First, through a spirit of disappointment and then through a spirit of adultery. Resist the enemy with my promises in my word. Praise me by faith for what I am about to do for the two of you. For it is the Lord that heals the broken in heart. It is the Lord that opens prison doors. It is the Lord that fulfills the deepest needs for human and physical love.

Yes, was not Gideon small in strength, yet I saw him a mighty man of valor? Was it not I the Lord that equipped him and gave him the courage to be the man I saw him to be? Yes, my children, I see the two of you the same way. A strong man of faith with strength and power. A strong woman of love with temperance in all things.

Stand upon my word, my children, and I will set your marriage free. I will heal. I will restore what the cankerworm tried to eat away. Did not David my servant err in a moment of weakness? Yet I took him back when he came to me. He was a man after my own heart. I do not see you as man would see you. I see the heart; two children of mine, lost for a time, but looking for something more in me.

I will bless you. I will set you free. I will move in by my Spirit on your situation. Praise my name and my word. For I am about to do a new thing for you. Wait on the Lord. Be of good courage and he will strengthen your heart. Your song will be a new song. A song of praise and deliverance unto my name.

> *Finally, be strong in the Lord and in his mighty power. Put on the full amour of God so that you can take your stand against the devil's schemes. For our struggle is not against flesh and blood, but against the rulers, against the authorities, against the powers of this dark world and against the spiritual forces of evil in the heavenly realm.* Ephesians 6:10-12

ADULTERY

DO YOU NEED HEALING

I have heard your heart cry. I have seen your heavy spirit as though loneliness would overtake you. But I say unto you, I have not appointed death, but life. Rise in me. Look to the cross. As my people of old looked to the serpent in the wilderness, so look to me, in faith, in life. As you look to me, you shall rise with hope, vigor, strength and new vision.

My healing wings are not withheld from your situation. Have faith in me. Have faith in me. I will speak unto you a word, and you shall rise and you shall go and you shall know that it is the Lord your God that sets the captives free.

> *Go back and tell Hezekiah, the leader of my people, This is what the Lord, the God of your father David, says: I have heard your prayer and seen your tears; I will heal you. On the third day from now you will go up to the temple of the Lord.* II Kings 20:5

AFFLICTION

IS GOD CALLING YOU TO TEACH

I have a call upon your life, a new vision and a new endeavor. As my Spirit moves you away from the shore into deeper waters of truth, I will teach you new things and you will teach others, with authority, my word. The authority you will have will not come by the inflection of your voice, but by my anointing.

Walk before me with all of your heart. Give up what is not of me. Serve me with all of your heart, soul and mind. I will bless you. I will bring you unto a broad path. This path will be firm in me. As you hunger after me, I will fill you up to overflowing with my Spirit.

In these latter days, I am raising up men and women to tread upon serpents, scorpions, and on all the power of the enemy. As you raise up my word, strongholds and demonic kingdoms will be cast asunder. I have chosen you. I have chosen you. Be faithful, even unto death and I will give you a crown of life.

> *The Sovereign Lord has given me an instructed*
> *tongue, to know the word that sustains the weary.*
> *He wakens me morning by morning, wakens my*
> *ear to listen like one being taught.*   Isaiah 50:4

AUTHORITY

HAVE YOU BEEN AWAY FROM GOD

I f you will hearken unto my voice to be careful to do all that I command you, I will bless you and restore unto you all the years of the locust. If you will hearken unto my voice to surrender your life completely to me, all that Satan has sought to steal from you, I will restore. Even from your earliest youth, I have called you. Though Satan has stolen you for a time, I will have you back. You are bought with a price, a price of redemption, the price of my blood.

You will return unto me weeping, but afterwards you will have joy, like that of a little child, bouncy and free. What was devastated in your home and in your person, I will restore. You will be wealthy, wealthy in me. What the cancer worm ate away, I will restore unto you one-hundred fold.

You will be a man of strength in me. You will teach my words to many. People will be set free, for the testimony that will flow out of your mouth will minister to others. My words will flow through you and you will rise with new vigor, for it will come from me.

I have seen his ways, but I will heal him; I will guide him and restore comfort to him, creating praise on the lips of the mourners in Israel. Peace, peace, to those far and near, says the Lord. And I will heal them.   Isaiah 57:18-19

BACKSLIDDEN

ARE YOU SENT OUT TOGETHER

I am intertwining your hearts. I am blending you together. I am forming a two-fold arm of strength and valor. Do not think it strange that you sense my love flowing through you to one another in a fresh way, a way you had not expected. I will blend your spirits as one, for a great exploit is ahead of you. You shall weep together. You shall laugh. You shall be amazed. But when it is finished, you will look back upon the path I chose for the two of you and will say, "that is why we were led together."

> *Calling the Twelve to him (Jesus), he sent them out two by two and gave them authority over evil spirits.*   Mark 6:7

BLENDING

IS SATAN TRYING TO KEEP YOU FROM CHURCH

You are coming up against Satanic oppression and opposition because of your zeal for the Lord. You are to stand on my Word, use my weapons of warfare in Ephesians 6:10-19, bind the enemy of confusion in the name of Jesus and loose the Spirit of peace. Ask that my angels guard you in all of your ways. (Psalms 91)

Be single-minded, that no matter what feelings or arguments come your way, you are going to church and to Bible study. (James 1:1-8)

When the enemy knows you are serious with your commitment and confession of my Word, he will back off. You have, through Christ, the power to destroy the strongholds of Satan against your home. (II Corinthians 10:4-6) You must take the weapons of Ephesians 6, walk in obedience and then stand upon my Word. Do not be discouraged if this takes time. Victory will come as you hold on. (I John 5:4-5) Satan has to relinquish his hold on the territory. The reason I came was to destroy the works of the devil. (I John 3:8) Believe this!

> *Jesus said to him, "Away from me, Satan! For it is written: 'Worship the Lord your God, and serve him only.'" Then the devil left him, and angels came and attended him.*   Matthew 4:10-11

BUFFETING

IS THIS A SPECIAL DAY

I want you to know that I love you. I love you. I love you. I bring to you encouragement, hope and deliverance on this your special day. Soon we will see each other and we will embrace and I will hold you. Crying will be no more, for I the Lord wipe away all tears and heal all your hurt. I am Jehovah, the God of all redemption, deliverance and healing.

Rise now with faith in your heart for what I say, I will do. What is not seen, will come into existence, for it is done, it is done, it is done.

> *And I heard a loud voice from the throne saying,*
> *'Now the dwelling of God is with men, and he will*
> *live with them. They will be his people, and God*
> *himself will be with them and be their God. He*
> *will wipe every tear from their eyes. There will*
> *be no more death or mourning or crying or pain,*
> *for the old order of things has passed away.'*
>
> Revelation 21:4

COMFORT

IS GOD ASKING YOU TO TRUST YOUR HUSBAND

Your spirit is anxious about many things. Sit at my feet. Draw from my wells and from your innermost being will flow strength, courage and stamina. I love you, my child. I am aware of your deepest distresses, and deepest needs. Yes, you have been fighting the forces of evil, the hosts of hell. But I am ready to do a new thing. Do you not perceive it? Can you not tell? My spirit and my angels are already in line to deliver, to set free, to move in on your situation.

Your husband is unto me as a chosen vessel. My spirit is at work even now to move, to draw, to bring forth fruit in his life for my use. Trust him, my child. Trust him as you would me, for my spirit is preparing you even now for the days ahead.

The unknown is often fearful. But when my glory is there, peace will come. Praise me my child. Take your eyes off yourself and put them on me; all of your affections, all of your desires, and all of your hopes. Put them on me and me alone. Offer a sacrifice of praise. Sing unto me a new song. When the glory of my presence is there, Satan flees for he cannot stay where there is holiness.

Praise me! Praise me! Praise me! All will work out for my glory. I am returning soon for my glorious bride, dipped in my blood and shining with the garments of praise. I will change your spirit of heaviness into joy. Just praise me with your whole being and I will move, work and bless.

I will speak a word here and there. You will know it for I will speak with encouragement, hope, deliverance and life. I am moving! I am moving! Rejoice in the God of your salvation who has delivered you from the past, out of bondage and has brought you into the refreshing waters of my Spirit.

> *Like an apple tree among the trees of the forest is my lover among the young men. I delight to sit in his shade and his fruit is sweet to my taste. He has taken me to the banquet hall, and his banner over me is love.* Song of Solomon 2:3-4

CONFIDENCE

DO YOU NEED DIRECTION

The Lord your God will direct you wherever you go. Turn not to the left, nor to the right, for I will show you the way and you will walk in it.

Obstacles will come, but I will overcome all by my word. Frustrations will mount up, but I will ease the difficulty with my presence. The task that is set before you is a great task. It is a task of power and might. The task that is set before you is difficult, but prayer will break the bonds. Do not fear what lies before you, for the time and place are set by me. Do not walk in unbelief, for faith in me will set the captives free. When your faith fails, my faith remains the same and will revive you.

Walk forward! Walk straight! Walk tall in me!

If the Lord delights in a man's way, he makes his steps firm; though he stumble, he will not fall, for the Lord upholds him with his hand.

Psalm 37:23-24

CONFIRMATION

DO YOU HAVE A MOTHER'S HEART

I say unto you, oh women of God, I have seen your heart's desire and it shall be fulfilled. Weep no more. Do not cry, for I see even into the deepest needs of your spirit. I see and I will bless you for your love and faithfulness to me in spite of your own affliction. You will rise a new woman in me; a woman of authority, of the Father's strength and will.

I have called you out amongst women from your earliest youth. I saw you when you played with your dolls. I saw a sweet spirit, a mother's heart. I the Lord saw all of this and it is I who have placed within you my sweet spirit of love for others. That love from me will grow now even more than ever before. You will rise with a ministry of Agape love. Women will come to you and receive the fresh waters of my Spirit of life. For your light affliction works for you an exceeding weight of glory.

Take heart! Rise with hope! Rise with faith! Rise with me and walk between the wings of the Cherubim, between the wings of my peace. I am Jehovah Nissi, your banner. I am Jehovah Mkaddesh, your righteousness.

> *As one whom his mother comforts, so I will comfort you. Blessed be the God and Father of our Lord Jesus Christ, the Father of mercies and God of all comfort, who comforts us in all our affliction, so that we may be able to comfort those who are in any affliction, with the comfort with*

which we ourselves are comforted by God. For as we share abundantly in Christ's sufferings, so through Christ we share abundantly in comfort too.   Isaiah 66:13A & II Corinthians 1:3-5

CONSOLING

DO YOU NEED ENCOURAGEMENT

Y ou are anxious about many things. I know your heart's secrets and what you desire the most. My child, I have seen the many tears that you have shed upon your bed. I have seen your many tears that have fallen on the sidewalk, along the roadway and as you have walked by the wayside. I have seen you when you were in despair, when you thought no one would come to your aid. But I the Lord have always been there, even when my Spirit baptized you. I was there endowing you with great strength so that you could face hardships, difficulties and trials. I have never forsaken you. I have always been there, faithful unto you in all things.

Trust me my child, for I the Lord am moving. Do not give in to despair, for the victory is just around the corner. Yes, you have been battling Satan's army, but I am greater. I am the victor. It is I who conquers the enemy as my people raise my Word and walk by faith. What you see with the natural eye will bring discouragement and loss of faith. But look deep within and see the way I see things, with spiritual insights and visions. I give hope. I give faith. I give the victory.

Hold on! Hold on! Hold on! Do not give territory to the evil one, for it is my will to save all. Hold on to my Word. Walk by faith. Pray on through no matter how long it takes. The ways of the world can be attractive, but I Am that I Am, a God of beauty when you see me in all things.

I have seen your faithfulness and I am pleased. I have seen your desire to see others come to know me, and I am moved. I have seen your hopes and aspirations crumble when Satan has flung a dart, but "greater is He that is in you than he that is in the world." (I John 4:4) Faith in me and my Word will conquer the greatest foe and bring victory in the greatest defeat. I am the Lord Jehovah, the God of Israel, the God who loves you. Believe, believe, believe. "Believe on the Lord Jesus Christ and you shall be saved and your whole household." (Acts 16:31)

> *I will go before you and will level the mountains.*
> *I will break down gates of bronze and cut through*
> *bars of iron. I will give you the treasures of dark-*
> *ness, riches stored in secret places, so that you*
> *may know that I am the Lord, the God of Israel,*
> *who summons you by name.*   Isaiah 45:2-3

COURAGE

DO YOU NEED CREATIVE IDEAS

I am the Lord that builds. I am the Lord that plants. I am the Lord that blossoms forth the fully budded tree. I am the Lord that brings forth fruit, for its season, for its time, and for its productivity.

I am the Lord that strengthens. I am the Lord that delivers all who come to me in faith believing. I am the Lord that sets free and opens the prison doors of all Satan's captives. It is I who does all these things.

Trust me! Trust me! Trust me! I bring organization to my children. I bring creative ideas. I am a God of great creativity. I will never let you down. I will never let you go. I will never move from my place. Claim my word of hope and deliverance for your situation.

When you were but a child, I knew you, picked you out and guided you. You are my chosen vessel and I love you. I love you. I have seen your tears fall upon the floor. I have seen your heart when it was breaking. I have seen you move with compassion for the children of men. Yes, my spirit is upon you in all of your ways and I am setting you completely free of remembering the pain of the past. As far as the East is from the West, so far have I removed your transgressions. My blood covers all. My blood washes all sins away. I make all things new.

In the days ahead, I will move upon your spirit and soul with a greater anointing. Ideas will pour forth to you and out of you.

You will say, "Where did that come from?" Know this my child, I AM sent them and give glory to me and me alone, lest the idea be taken and given to another.

Your weeping will be turned to joy for I will give to you the joy of my Spirit. You will sing. You will dance. You will extend your hands in praise to me and I will be blessed, blessed, blessed by it. For are we not one, joined in spirit to bring glory and honor to my name?

Your children and your household are blessed by me. Prove me to see whether or not the windows of heaven will pour forth a blessing. I will bless you. I will bless you. I will bless you. I love you my child. I am Jehovah Shammah. I am present wherever you go. I am Jehovah Shalom. I am the God of all peace.

> *He who forms the mountains, creates the wind,*
> *and reveals his thoughts to man, he who turns*
> *dawn to darkness, and treads the high places of*
> *the earth—-the Lord God Almighty is his name.*
>
> Amos 4:13

CREATIVITY

ARE YOU COMING TO A CROSSROAD

I the Lord, your God, see the crossroads. I the Lord Jehovah see your perplexing situation. Did I not say to you that I will never leave you nor forsake you? I deliver all who call on me. I deliver all who stand upon my word and believe it.

Did I not say to you to walk upon the chosen road, the road of peace? Do not be confused. Satan seeks to rob you of my direction. I will not let you go. I will brighten up the path, making it more clear, more plain, making it like crystal. Yes, you will see my direction and my plan. It will be plain to you.

I love you. I have seen your tears and your anxiety. I have seen your concerns. But remember that I am greater than any opposing force. I have a new work for you to do. The old is passed. The new has come and you are being made ready to walk upon that new path.

Have faith in me and my word. The waters will part. You will walk between the wings of the cherubim and you will walk with me on dry ground. Do not fear. At the acceptable time I will visit you. I will speak and you will know my leading.

> *What you decide on will be done, and light will shine on your ways....He restores my soul. He guides me in paths of righteousness for his name's sake.* Job 22:28 & Psalm 23:3

DECISIONS

HAVE YOU FAILED

Is anything too hard to me to do? Is anything too hard for me to bring the victory? Yield to me. Yield to me. Failure in anything is my opportunity for success and growth. Failure is my opportunity to make strong what is weak.

Yield to my Spirit. Put aside all awareness of the natural senses, for I flow out of yielded vessels, pure and clear water from the inner most being, that it might give life to all around.

Your mourning will be turned to laughter. Your failure is my success. Your lack is my strength flowing through you. Keep your thoughts out of the realm of my Spirit, for my Spirit does not flow out of the mind, but out of the inner most being. My Spirit is like a bubbling brook, pouring forth from the deepest well inside, transforming and renewing the mind. Yes, my Spirit will be upon you in the days ahead. Be obedient in all things and I will bless, bless, bless.

> *Jesus replied, what is impossible with men is possible with God.*   Luke 18:27

DEFEAT

ARE YOU IN DEPRESSION

Oh soul, why are you in such distress? Oh soul, why do you weep? Do you not know that the Lord, the Creator of the universe does not tarry, nor is He slack concerning His promises? The God that called you out amongst my people sees your distress and your anguish of heart. Do you suppose for one moment that I do not know what Satan is trying to do to you my child? I know every scheme, every wile, and every harassment. Yes, Satan does seek to devour you. But I am greater and mightier than any oppressive force, and victory is at your right hand. My hand of power, my hand of praise, shall be exalted above your position, above your situation. Satan will flee with but a breath of my power and word.

Soul, do not weep, or mourn, or cry. My Covenant of peace will go with you in all my paths of life. My covenant of promise will be established. I am a Mighty God. I am an All-Powerful God.

Trust me! Trust me! Trust me! I am moving even now to break the fetters asunder, the cords of Sheol (death), and the cords of bondage. Satan will not have the victory over you in your home, on the job, or wherever you go. He is abased, defeated and I the Lord exalted in you. I give to you my fullness, my joy and my life.

The Lord will rescue me from every evil attack and will bring me safely to his heavenly kingdom. To Him be glory for ever and ever. Amen.

II Timothy 4:18

DEPRESSION

ARE YOU CONFUSED

I have not forgotten you, my child. I have not let you down. As my Spirit has moved upon you, I have called you forth. I have called you out. As my Spirit has moved upon you, I have called you to a wider path, a firmer path, a path of love and truth in me.

Yes, many doubts have crept in on you, many diverse ways of thinking. But I am stabilizing you, my child. I am calling you to a greater consecration, a greater dedication to my will and purposes in your life. As you obey my leading in all things and walk by faith, I will bring you to Canaan, the Promised Land. Leave the past to me. Leave the present to me. Leave the future to me. As you trust me in all things, I will bless you. I will bless your whole household, for you are a sanctifying element in it.

You have felt many hurts, but as you make reconciliation with those whom I will reveal to you, blessings will abound. Satan will not have victory over you. As you put my word first in all things, upholding the word of truth and my name, I will bring you into abundant blessing and wealth in me. I see your heart, my child, and how it longs to be set free in all things. Even now I am bringing inner healing to your soul, to your mind, emotions and will.

I have seen your desire to be used by me, and you will be used by me. As you obey my leading in all things, my Spirit will pour forth out of you in a new and mighty way. Others in your household will say, "What has happened!" As you walk with me, they will be set free, too. I love you my child. Hold your head high in me for I am the lifter up of your head.

> *But the land you are crossing the Jordan to take*
> *possession of is a land of mountains and valleys*
> *that drinks rain from heaven. It is a land the Lord*
> *your God cares for; the eyes of the Lord your*
> *God are continually on it from the beginning of*
> *the year to its end.* Deuteronomy 11:11-12

DIRECTION

IS GOD TRAINING YOU

T he Word of the Lord says, *Be anxious for nothing, but in everything by prayer and supplication with thanksgiving let your requests be made known unto God.* (Philippians 4:6) The Word of the Lord also says, *Let not your heart be troubled, believe in God, believe also in me. In my Father's house are many dwelling places. If it were not so, I would have told you. I go away and prepare a place for you, that where I am there you may be also.* (John 14:1-2)

My Word, my child, is a lamp unto your feet and a light unto your path. Study it with all of your heart and I will speak to you. I will reveal myself to you. I see your troubled heart and I am moved with compassion. I see your desire to be used by me. I see your desire to be meek, to be humble, to not go ahead of my leading, but to follow my voice. And yes, you are hearing me correctly. It is I, the Shepherd that goes before you even now and prepares the way for the Lord to be manifested through you. Yes, your hungry spirit will be satisfied, your thirsty mouth, quenched, and your desire to be used, not half but fully, in ministry.

Do not doubt what I have revealed to you so far. Walk in faith, believing me. As you take my shield and my sword, Satan cannot touch you. Even he will flee with but a breath of my word going forth; for it will not be your breath, but my breath of life coming out of you.

Rise, take courage. What I have been preparing you for is almost here. Did not I train my servant Moses in the wilderness? Did not I train Jacob in the wilderness? Yes, some of my choicest leaders have been trained in the wilderness, in the hot desert. But when they have come out of the desert, they have come with rods of leadership and correction to my people. They have come out with staffs of victory and might.

I know your wilderness, but I have walked with you my child, each step of the way. When you have felt the burning desert sand under your feet, my spirit has been there to cool you, to deliver you. Be patient, unmovable and abound in my work. Though what might seem insignificant to others, in my eyes it is a refreshing flood of water, of praise unto me. Walk in faith. Live in me and fruitful you will be.

> *In a desert land he found him, in a barren and howling waste. He shielded him and cared for him; he guarded him as the apple of his eye.*
>
> Deuteronomy 32:10

DISCIPLINE

HAS GOD EXPANDED YOUR MINISTRY

My anointing is truly upon you. My anointing is truly moving you out. As the sun shines on a bright clear day, so my light is within you and upon you. I have chosen you from the womb. I have preserved you for this hour, this day, and this time. The Spirit of the Lord moves in ways that are not always understood, so my Spirit moves you in ways that others cannot understand.

Do not go back into Egypt. Do not go back into bondage; no never, no never, no never. Let my Spirit keep moving you forward in new ways and in new territories for my glory.

Before you lies a wide-open green field with flowers ready to bloom. This is a wide open field of grain, a wide open field of ministry. From this day forward, you shall know my anointing, my power, my leading as the sands of the sea, as the stars of the heaven. It will abound in you, on top of you, underneath your feet, and all around you. For the Lord your God has set you free to minister in Jerusalem, Judea and to the uttermost parts of my earth. You have been faithful in little things. I will now put you over much.

The enemy is around. He is always lurking to destroy, to take the humble in spirit and make proud. Stay faithful to me and know that my anointing flows through full obedience and love for others, without respect of persons. I love you. I have much for you to accomplish. Walk humbly, hand in hand, in one spirit with God. I love you, says the Spirit of Grace.

You will go out in joy and be led forth in peace; the mountains and hills will burst into song before you, and all the trees of the field will clap their hands. Instead of the thorn bush will grow the pine tree, and instead of briers, the myrtle will grow. This will be for the Lord's renown, for an everlasting sign, which will not be destroyed. Isaiah 55:12-13

EXPANSION

ARE YOU WORRIED ABOUT YOUR DAUGHTER

I am not finished with you yet. My Spirit has anointed you for leadership in the past, and I will again anoint you even more for new paths and new leadership. I have seen your faithfulness against obstacles, and I am pleased. I have seen your love, and I am moved. I have seen your cry for me to use you, and I will do just that.

I have been preparing you. Though the training has been rough and hard, I have never let you down. I will never forsake you. You are bought with my precious blood. Rise with my name on your lips and it will break bondages. Rise and declare my blood, and souls will be won for my kingdom.

I am returning soon and my Spirit will be calling forth your daughter to rise with new courage and new hope in me. I am taking away from her the years of the locust. I am placing before her an abundant life in me. She shall be loved! She shall be loved! She will know a new anointing that she has not sensed before. A calling is on her to follow me.

Walk before me humbly. Honor me with all that I give to you and I will multiply it and multiply it again. I am moving quickly and swiftly over the face of the earth. I am returning soon. I will be giving you a fresh vision and a fresh awareness of my word. You will hunger for it. You will crave it. Revelation knowledge will come to you and my word will go forth. My word will be declared. My word will be performed.

*Pass through, pass through the gates! Prepare
the way for the people. Build up, build up the
highway! Remove the stones. Raise a banner for
the nations. The Lord has made proclamation to
the ends of the earth: Say to the Daughter of Zion,
'See your Savior comes! See, his reward is with
him, and his recompense accompanies him.'.*

Isaiah 62:10-11

EXPECTATIONS

ARE YOU CONTEMPLATING BUILDING

I have seen your heart. I have seen your desire to seek me with all of your heart. I have seen your contriteness, repentance, tears and groaning. I have seen all these things and yes, I will answer you. I will visit at the acceptable time. I will move. Why do you doubt? Have I not brought you through many wildernesses? Have I not fed you with the manna from heaven, and with fresh, living water? Nothing is too hard for me. Nothing is too difficult for me. I will answer. I will pour out my spirit in a fresh living way. Though there are those who come, and those who go, yet am I not a God that never leaves you or forsakes you?

Weep no more, neither mourn, for I want your praise. Praise me for who I am and what I have done and what I will do. Even as Nehemiah was used by me to build the walls of Jerusalem and preserve a remnant, so you shall be used to build my Kingdom. Others will come within the gates of my building and be set free in body and in spirit. Life shall flow, my clear living water, my oil, my manna, my praise. Do not fret. I am mighty to supply every need, so much so that you will call unto me in the day of visitation and say, "It is enough, for truly I have seen your salvation."

*I also told them about the gracious hand of my
God upon me and what the king had said to me.
They replied, Let us start rebuilding. So they
began this good work.* Nehemiah 2:18

EXPLOITS

ARE YOU LOOKING FOR YOUR FAMILY
TO BE USED

S et your priorities in order. Give me first place in all things and obey me wherever I send you. I love you and my Spirit is drawing you into deeper springs, yes into the river of my Spirit and my word. Even now it is flowing forth to you.

My return is soon and the talent I have placed within you will blossom with much fruit in the days and years ahead. I have chosen you and your family to minister, to minister, to minister for my glory.

Do not be anxious about anything. Submit all to me and I will move upon the hearts of all your loved ones. Speak positively, in love as I go before you to prepare the way. Listen for the inner voice of my Spirit.

> *For I will pour water on the thirsty land, and streams on the dry ground; I will pour out my Spirit on your offspring, and my blessing on your descendants. They will spring up like grass in a meadow, like poplar trees by flowing streams.*
> Isaiah 44:3-4

FAMILY

DO YOU NEED FORGIVENESS

I am a God of great forgiveness, great mercy and great compassion. Hide my word in your heart and I will call it forth when my Spirit moves upon you. My love and my banner will be raised for you against any flood of bad memories. I wipe away the past. I remember it no more. Your love for me is like a beautiful tree in full bloom. You are being made ready, by my Spirit, to bear much fruit for my kingdom, and for my glory.

> *As far as the east is from the west, so far has he removed our transgressions from us. As a father has compassion on his children, so the Lord has compassion on those who fear him.*

Psalms 103:12-13

FORGIVENESS

DO YOU NEED A BREAKTHROUGH

I t is the Lord your God who gladdens the hearts of his servants. It is the Lord your God who sets the captives free. It is the Lord your God who quickens you to move out by my Spirit. I am doing new things in your life. I am doing new, great and marvelous things in you. I am moving you out with new ideas and in new ways that are unfamiliar to you. But it is the Lord your God who is doing these things.

Yes, you are being set free. The oppression you have been feeling has not come from me but rather from the evil one, the powers of darkness that would seek to destroy you. I the Lord move in peace and in unity, not in strife, confusion or misunderstandings. It is the Lord that has called you into this place, at this time, to do this work for me.

I know your feelings of inadequacy. Yes, I know that you have been fighting the forces of evil. But my dear child, as my word is raised and as you praise me, those forces leave. Holiness cannot dwell with evil and evil with holiness, for they are contrary to one another.

Lift up your voice and praise me with all your heart, soul and mind. I need that sacrifice of praise. I will come upon you and anoint you for service with ideas that come from my Spirit within you.

I hear your heart's desire. I hear your frequent intercession and I am pleased with you. My child, you have been chosen from the womb and though Satan has had you for a time, I have you now and all the past is gone and is forgiven. I see a pure vessel with great potential for my glory.

Serve me with all your heart, with all your soul and with all your might. I am giving you a breakthrough. I am inundating you with power from on high. The feelings of insecurity around others, and the lack of ideas, will all be changed with my anointing. I have visited you and I am doing great and mighty things throughout the earth.

Commit your ways to me, trust in me and I will bring it to pass. I supply all of your needs. Those great financial needs will be met by my power. Claim my word. Talk in faith. Speak to the mountain.

I see you new and glorious, dancing before many for my glory; setting others free because I have set you free with a new song to be sung unto me.

I am coming soon for a glorious bride without spot and wrinkle. Watch and see the salvation of the Lord as you praise and intercede. Hold on my child. Your prayers will be answered for before you spoke them, I sent the answer on the way. You will rise with new courage, hope and endeavors for my kingdom.

> *Let the saints rejoice in this honor and sing for joy on their beds. May the praise of God be in their mouths, and a double-edged sword in their hands.* Psalms 149:5-6

FREEDOM

ARE YOU TOO OLD FOR GOD TO USE

I say unto you, you have my wisdom from my word. You have a surrendered heart. You have been walking on a lighted path. But I would say unto you, seek me anew with your whole heart. Seek me in a different way, in a way of an exploit in me. For as my sheep grow, I lead them to greener pastures of love and surrender. Yes, I lead beside still waters, but waters of great power.

I see into your heart. I see into your spirit. I know things you have not seen yet. Yes, my child, I want you to see them too. I want you to know them; for as my Spirit moves upon you, you will be like Sarah of old. You will bear fruit in your old age. This fruit will be of great magnitude for my kingdom. I do not see age. I see life; life that is willing to come forth and follow me; life that is willing to say, "I will serve you to the end!"

Trust me my child, for my anointing upon you will give you strength, hope and courage. Follow me now! Follow me and be set free in a new way.

> *The righteous will flourish like a palm tree; they*
> *will grow like a cedar of Lebanon; planted in the*
> *house of the Lord, they will flourish in the courts*
> *of our God. They will still bear fruit in old age,*
> *they will stay fresh and green, proclaiming, 'The*
> *Lord is upright, he is my Rock and there is no*
> *wickedness in him'.* Psalms 92:12-15

FRUITFULNESS

ARE YOUR DESIRES FULFILLED

I have seen your heart, my child. I have seen your longings. I have seen your desires, and I am moved. My Spirit is moving, is calling, and is drawing all who are open to him. And I see, my child, that your heart is open, your emotions are open, your spirit and your mind are ready to receive all I have for you. Yes, you will be fulfilled in all things. The desires of your heart will be answered. Your deepest longings will be satisfied. For my Spirit brings life in fullness, in joy and in abundance.

> *May he give you the desire of your heart and make your plans succeed. We will shout for joy when you are victorious and will lift up our banners in the name of our God. May the Lord grant all your requests.* Psalm 20:4-5

FULFILLMENT

IS GOD USING THE TWO OF YOU

I say unto you my servants, you have not yet seen and witnessed what I want to do through the two of you. A new day is about to dawn upon your ministry. What was done yesterday is gone. What is going to be done today is here. Yes, you will hear my thunderous voice, my voice of strength, and my roaring voice. A great, great wave of my Spirit is ready to pour out upon your ministry. New healings will take place; new words of faith will come forth; new hope will be given to those who are in bondage. I will pour upon you revelation knowledge from my word. This will be knowledge you have not known before. Do you ever suppose to understand all of me? Even in the jot and tittle there is truth to unfold, and there is knowledge of the great I AM, for I AM that I AM!

> *The voice of the Lord is over the water; the God of glory thunders, the Lord thunders over the mighty waters. The voice of the Lord is powerful; the voice of the Lord is majestic. The voice of the Lord breaks the cedars; the Lord breaks in pieces the cedars of Lebanon. The voice of the Lord strikes with flashes of lightening. The voice of the Lord shakes the desert; the Lord shakes the Desert of Kadesh. The voice of the Lord twists the oaks and strips the forests bare. And in his temple all cry, "GLORY".* Psalms 29:3-5 & 7-9

GOD'S VOICE

DO YOU BELIEVE YOUR MINISTRY IS OVER

My Son, My Son:

I know your deepest hurt, deepest distress, deepest want and deepest desire. Know this my boy, I have seen you when you have faltered. I have seen you when you have been strong. I have seen you when you have said, "Why go on? What for? I have nothing to live for. Nothing is left." Know this my son, you are mine. I have bought you, redeemed your life and given you my Holy Spirit. Nothing, no nothing, no nothing will stop my blessings from flowing to you when you walk hand in hand with me. I still have much ministry ahead for you, much life, much joy and much fulfillment.

I don't care how much Satan has sought to take your life, your love and your very breathe. He is not victorious. I AM. I am the Almighty God who plucks up and casts down. The ground that Satan has taken from you, turn over to me in faith believing my word. I will set you free. I will give you new life. All the evil, which Satan sought to do to you, will become a cluster of fruit; a life giving perfect tree, bearing much, much, much for my Glory.

I have chosen for you a new course in life. Leave the past behind. Go on to what is new. I don't expect perfection in my servants, but obedience and availability. Walk in the light of my Glory. I will reveal to you your new course, your new path, and all will be fresh and alive because I am alive.

I live in you my son. I love you. I love you. I love you. Your tears will flow with joy to me when you see what I have in store for you. Walk in faith. Speak my word. I am a God of deliverance and of Grace. Your work and faithfulness is not forgotten. It will be rewarded. Praise my name!

> *The Lord had said to Abram, 'leave your country, your people and your father's household and go to the land I will show you. I will make you into a great nation and I will bless you; I will make your name great, and you will be a blessing. I will bless those who bless you, and whoever curses you, I will curse; and all peoples on earth will be blessed through you.' So Abram left, as the Lord had told him; and Lot went with him. Abram was seventy-five years old when he set out from Haran.* Genesis 12: 1-4

GOING FORWARD

ARE YOU AFRAID TO TRUST GOD

I want to address the men of my body. When you were little boys, your mother would take you by the hand and lead you around from place to place. Then the day came for you to leave your mother's side and go to school. For some of you this was very traumatic. For others, this was a very lonely time. And still for others, this was quite peaceful, quite matter-of-fact. Men, some of you however, have not let go. You are still holding on to mother's hand in the school yard. You don't want to grow up emotionally and spiritually. I'm working by my Spirit to bring you into greater responsibilities, greater spiritual understanding, but you refuse to follow. You are afraid to trust Me.

I need men today, men who will pay the price of servant-hood, men who will pay the price of obedience, men who will pay the price of love. Love me men. I have so much I want to give you, but so often my hand is blocked.

Give up what is not of my leading. Let your ambitions and desires be turned to me and I will bless you beyond your imagination. Your business will increase, your children brought back to me, your wife will be to you a lover, a help-meet. I'm not a cruel taskmaster, but I do require your full attention and your full obedience.

Give me your money. Yes, give me back my money and I will bless one-hundred fold in ways you have not asked for.

I have so much for you. Just trust me. Let go of the old ways. Seek what is new and I will move you, I will bless you, I will honor you and your whole household. Trust me and see the windows of heaven shower down blessing, blessings, and more blessings. Take up the cross and follow me today.

> *Surely God is my salvation; I will trust and not be afraid. The Lord, the Lord, is my strength and my song; he has become my salvation. With joy you will draw water from the wells of salvation. In that day you will say: 'Give thanks to the Lord, call on his name; make known among the nations what he has done, and proclaim that his name is exalted. Sing to the Lord, for he has done glorious things; let this be known to all the world.'* Isaiah 12:2-5

GROWING UP

DOES YOUR MINISTRY NEED GROWTH

M y Spirit is upon you. As I move, you will sense rising within a greater anointing, a greater power. The ministry I have for you is ordained by me. Though Satan has sought to tear you apart, I mend all, I deliver, I heal and I set free. As you move out with my authoritative power, speculations, vain imaginations, schisms, are all put down.

Hold on to my word. Stand upon it. I am Captain of the ship. Hold the stern, the rudder in place under my direction and my leadership. The ministry will grow and be blessed. Though opposition may come, I shall weed out who is not ready to receive and who is not ready to grow. I will bless and I will multiply. Do not be surprised. My Word will divide soul and spirit. My Word will go forth in anointed power, under my direction. You will rise with new thoughts, new revelation and you will know that the Lord God gave it to you. Have faith in me. Have faith in me. Have faith in me.

Every day they continued to meet together in the temple courts. They broke bread in their homes and ate together with glad and sincere hearts. Praising God and enjoying the favor of all the people. And the Lord added to their number daily those who were being saved. Acts 2:46-47

GROWTH

ARE YOU SEEKING ANOINTED GUIDANCE

I say unto you, "eyes have not seen, nor ears heard, nor has it entered into your heart all I have prepared for you." For as my Spirit moves upon you in the days and months ahead, I will show you many thoughts, ideas and plans. I have led you in all your ways and I will continue to guide you in a greater way. Others around you will not understand my leading in your life. But as my Spirit moves, they will see unfolding a mighty plan, because I am pouring out on you an anointing for a greater exploit for my glory and honor.

This is a new day, a day of new beginnings, a day of a fresh anointing and revival of my Spirit. I have seen your faithfulness against great obstacles, against others who do not understand the leading of the Shepherd. I have seen you when you have cried into the wee hours of the morning for my will to be accomplished in your life. I have recorded all those tears and each one I have felt along with you as you have sought to take hold of my garment in prayer. Those tears have not gone unnoticed.

I am rewarding you. I am bringing you into great responsibility, into a greater move of my Spirit. The road that is before you is not an easy road, but it is an anointed road of power; a road of deliverance to captives; a road of healing to many of my wayward sheep. I am granting you discernment and wisdom to know paths of good and evil. As you go forth, you will know joy, victory and power, for I am anointing you before my people.

You shall rise with new words and with oracles. You will wonder where the words came from. But know this my child, those words came from me. Others will say, "Oh, my! Look what God has accomplished; look at what God has done!" For I am the Lord God mighty in visitation, in words, in deeds, steadfast in love, steadfast in discernment, steadfast in knowledge, steadfast in mercy, steadfast in compassion, steadfast in provision in all things. For I am Jehovah Shammah. I am present wherever you go. I am present with you now.

> *Whether you turn to the right or to the left, your ears will hear a voice behind you, saying, 'This is the way; walk in it.'*   Isaiah 30:21

GUIDANCE

DO YOU BELIEVE SATAN OR GOD

My Son:

I have heard your prayers and have seen you in your moments of distress. I want you to know that I love you and I want you to serve me. I still have great things in store for you. Do not listen to the taunts of Satan, for he is a liar and a father of all lies. I have forgiven you. I see your repentance. David sinned, and yes he repented. Yet I called him a man after my own heart. This is the way I look upon you.

Place your trust in me. Yes, trust only in me and take the authority of my word over the taunts of the evil one, in the name of my son Jesus. Let the guilt and the lie that you are not fit to serve me, roll off of you as water rolls off the back of a duck.

Draw close to me in prayer. Let my Holy Spirit renew your spirit and I will show you open doors that you did not know were even there. I love you and because of my son's blood, you, too, are my son.

Let the Holy Spirit soothe your wounded heart and soothe your hurts and fill you with my love. Abide in me and I will cause you to bear much fruit for my Kingdom. I will bless you more than you can ever imagine.

> *Therefore, there is now no condemnation for those who are in Christ Jesus, because through Christ Jesus the law of the Spirit of life set me free from the law of sin and death.*   Romans 8:1-2

GUILT FREE

IS YOUR HUSBAND DISCOURAGED

Y our husband shall rise with a banner of victory, with a banner of hope, and with my blood covering him with protection. Your husband is sanctified by my word. I have called him. I have set him apart, and you shall rise in victory with him. You will have a home of love, a love nest set apart for my glory.

I am the God of your situation. Weep no more. Do not fret. Do not shrink back in fear. Be obedient in all things. For my Spirit of life truly rests upon you. Your weeping will turn to joy, joy, joy. You will laugh. You will dance. You will sing a new song in the congregation of men for my glory.

Restore our fortunes, O lord, like streams in the Negev. Those who sow in tears will reap with songs of joy. He who goes out weeping carrying seed to sow, will return with songs of joy, carrying sheaves with him. Psalms 126:4-6

HOPE

DAUGHTER, IS GOD CALLING YOU TO MINISTER ENCOURAGEMENT

I have seen your tears of joy, sorrow and agony, and I am moved. Your tears are all recorded in my book. I have kept note of all of them. I am moved by your love for me. I have put within your heart and your spirit compassion, love, mercy and grace for the unloved, the wayward and those whom others would say to, "There is no hope."

I have anointed you to stand alongside of your husband. But I have also not forgotten your individuality. I have set before you ministry also; a ministry of encouragement and of hope to those who are feeling discouraged. Walk in it and be obedient in all things.

I know your feelings, your desires, and times of discouragement when you wonder, "Who am I"? Let it be known to you my daughter, that you are a princess in my eyes, a daughter of the King; therefore, no one who is royalty is ever insignificant.

I have saved you for this time. My Spirit will pour forth from you in new boldness, new love and new wisdom, in my name. My Spirit is upon the handmaidens of the Lord.

I love you my child and I am returning soon. I am raising women to be bold in me, prophetesses in my name. You are a chosen vessel and as my Spirit moves you in the days ahead, sing unto me a new song in the congregation of men. Prophecy in humility for it is the Lord your God that released you from the past and has set you free on a new path. Worship me in the beauty of who I am, in the beauty of holiness.

Therefore encourage one another, and build each other up, just as in fact you are doing.

I Thessalonians 5:11

INSPIRATION

ARE YOU LED TO PRAY FOR THE NATION

I, the Lord, am moving in a new and mysterious way over the face of the earth. I am moving and I am bringing the purging fires into every public place. I am moving into every area from the smallest to the largest. I am moving. I am searching for vessels who are ready to move out by my Spirit into areas that have not seen my imprint thus far. For my Spirit is calling and there are those who are joining in the marching ranks of my mighty army. My Spirit has been leading and going before. Satan's hosts are trembling under the mighty wave of prayer. For in the heavenlies it is like a huge tidal wave, swishing demonic kingdoms down. For my church is rising to the position of authority I intended it to exercise. As more join in and pray, a great change will occur. A great move will take place.

Do not say in your heart, "Oh, but the Lord is returning. Why should I pray? Will not all be destroyed anyway?" I say unto you my child, you do not know the hour of my return. Did not I say, "Occupy until I come?" When you are not busy doing my work and allowing my purposes to be accomplished in your life, it is sin and you must repent.

Occupy my children. Be busy doing the work of the Father. Did not I listen and obey His commands? Likewise, my children listen and obey me in all things. Though you are small in number, a great harvest of souls will take place. Though you seem like a speck in the universe, yet I will bless your faithfulness. Danger is being averted. Satan's hosts trembling as they see you pray and intercede on behalf of the nation. Be faithful. Prayer is not a small thing in my sight, but a great thing. I love you. I love you. I love you.

> *I looked for a man among them who would build up the wall and stand before me in the gap on behalf of the land so I would not have to destroy it, but I found none....I urge then, first of all, that requests, prayers, intercession and thanksgiving be made for everyone—for kings and all those in authority, that we may live peaceful and quiet lives in all godliness and holiness. This is good, and pleases God our Savior, who wants all men to be saved and to come to a knowledge of the truth.* Ezekiel 22:30 & I Timothy 2:1-4

INTERCESSION

IS THE HOLY SPIRIT CALLING YOU

M y Spirit is moving swiftly upon the face of the earth calling here and calling there to those who will listen. My Spirit is moving swiftly upon the face of the earth, enlisting volunteers into the army of God. My Spirit is moving and calling to those who will obey me with all their heart, their soul and their mind. Yes, my Spirit is calling out a people of love, of deliverance, of fullness. For I, the Lord Jesus, am ready to return, to bring into reality my kingdom before all men, before all beings in the heavens above, the earth beneath and under the earth. I am doing a new thing, a new and wondrous thing to behold. Those who are open to my Spirit will experience my moving, my power and my deliverance in a way they have never known.

> *The Spirit and the bride say, Come! And let him who hears say, 'come!' Whoever is thirsty, let him come; and whoever wishes, let him take the free gift of the water of life.* Revelations 22:17

INVITATION

DO YOU WANT REVELATION KNOWLEDGE

The Lord God is moving and calling forth a bride who is purified by the water and the word. I am calling forth vessels who will flow with revelation knowledge from me. As I am moving upon vessels, I am calling forth my people to study and learn my word with a greater unction and power from on high. As my Spirit prompts, I am moving to bring about great truths to be revealed in these last days, hidden pearls in a treasure chest full of precious secrets of my kingdom.

Not all of my children will pay the price to rise early and get alone with me. Not all will pay the price to take time out from busy days to seek me. Not all will linger at my fountain of life at the night watches. But those in my kingdom who will follow me wholeheartedly, I will reveal myself wholeheartedly to and revelation knowledge from my word shall come forth.

I am returning soon for a bride without spot, cleansed by my blood, washed in my word, clean through and through. My people, "rise to greater heights of glory. Rise to greater exploits. Rise and be set free in me." As you learn from me, bondage's will go, sin blotted out, prison doors opened, marriages healed, finances met. All my secrets are within my word. Will you not pay the price to learn from me? Did I not pay the price for you? Follow me without reservation. I will bless you and show my goodness and my name to you.

I want you to know, brothers, that the gospel I preached is not something that man made up. I did not receive it from any man, nor was I taught it; rather I received it by revelation from Jesus Christ.   Galatians 1:11-12

KINGDOM SECRETS

ARE YOU WAITING FOR MARCHING ORDERS

Y ou are a leader, a leader among women. I am training you and preparing you even now for leadership in my kingdom. My Spirit shall flow thru you. My gifts will be demonstrated in your life.

As my Spirit leads you in the days ahead, I will be speaking to you with a word here and a word there. It will be confirmed by my anointed leadership and my written word. My Spirit is moving you out, to go forward to be a part of a mighty move of my Spirit. I am raising up an army, a prayer warrior army that will go forth with a banner of victory.

El Shaddai is my name. I am sufficient to meet every need in your life.

> *Deborah, a prophetess, the wife of Lappidoth, was leading Israel at that time. She held court under the Palm of Deborah between Ramah and Bethel in the hill country of Ephraim, and the Israelites came to her to have their disputes decided.*   Judges 4:4-5

LEADERSHIP/WOMEN

ARE YOU HOLDING ON TO THE PAST

L et go and let me work through you. Let go and I will bless you. Let go and I will multiply your resources, your blessings, your ministry. For as you let go of the past, I can move you forward. As you move out, trust me through the wilderness, through the desert of your life. I will bring you to an oasis, to the Promised Land. As you let go, my Spirit will open up the closed doors. There are many doors I have for you and many places for you to go.

I have seen your love and your faithfulness to me. I am very pleased with you. I have seen your desire to not hurt and let others down, and I am pleased. That love, that compassion comes from me. Surely as I move you into deeper waters, I will bless you. I will not let one little one be offended. I will not let one go. For I never leave you or forsake you. Trust in me with all of your heart, do not lean upon your own understanding; in all of your ways acknowledge me and I will direct your path. I am El Shaddai, the All-Sufficient One.

> *By faith Abraham when called to go to a place he would later receive as his inheritance, obeyed and went, even though he did not know where he was going. By faith he made his home in the Promised Land like a stranger in a foreign country; he lived in tents, as did Isaac and Jacob, who were heirs with him of the same promise. For he was looking forward to the city with foundations, whose architect and builder is God.* Hebrews 11:8-10

LETTING GO

ARE YOU IN FEAR OF DYING

The angel of death shall not alight upon your door step, for I have not appointed death, but life. You shall rise with new hope, new vigor and new strength. You shall know that you are loved by me, by others and by your family. I will be wooing and drawing you by my Spirit to the wells of salvation, and you will experience freedom and deliverance.

I know your heart. I know your desires. I know your fears. Fear will not overtake you. I am stabilizing your mind. I am stabilizing your body. I am stabilizing your home. I will speak to you new wisdom, new hope and new direction.

Love me with all of your heart, with all of your soul, and with all of your mind. I will move into your situation and do exceedingly abundantly above all that you can imagine. Your home shall prosper, for you are a sanctifying element and a hope to those around you. Rise now with new courage, my child, for I have appointed true life unto you and your whole household.

> *For you, O Lord, have delivered my soul from death, my eyes from tears, my feet from stumbling, that I may walk before the Lord in the Land of the living.*   Psalms 116:8-9

LIFE

ARE YOU IN TROUBLE

Weep no more my child. Weep no more. For I the Lord deliver you. I the Lord set you free. I the Lord give hope amidst the storm. Though the waters come up to your neck, they will not overflow you. Though the waters come up and try to drown you, my sustaining hand reaches down to yours. For I the Lord see you. I see all and I know all. And I Jesus, set you free, pick you up and put a new song on your lips. I Jesus bring you out of the mire. Even now my spirit is moving upon you to heal, to bind up that which is broken, to put in place what is lame.

I love you. I love you. I love you. I am doing a new thing in your life. Can you not perceive it? Can you not tell? For I see you like an eagle soaring high above the mountains into the sky. I see you like a flower, in full bloom, full of fragrance and beauty. I see you like a precious new born baby, all soft, pure and clean. That is the way I see you. Picture that within your spirit and you will be set free of all the past. I Jesus give you a new course, a new path and my light will make it plain to you in the days ahead.

Let me go before you in all things. You will know my leading for it will be through a whisper, a word, an anointed leader, and my Word. Some of my sheep get anxious for greener pastures, for higher mountains and they get caught in the bramble bushes and wolves try to devour them. But I will lead you softly, gently, with my Shepherd staff, with my rod of love, mercy and correction. Even now I am preparing for you a very special ministry of love, of hope to the hopeless, of healing to the broken in heart.

Do not be anxious about anything, but submit quietly all to me in prayer and I will go before you to open the doors, to prepare the way. Fear comes from the evil one. But I give you a sound mind. I give joy. I give life. In me there is no bondage, and no condemnation.

I am coming soon. Walk in faith, believe, stand firm, resist the devil and He will surely flee from you. My Word is your hope, your strength and your life.

> *Though I walk in the midst of trouble, you preserve my life; you stretch out your hand against the anger of my foes, with your right hand you save me.* Psalms 138:7

NEW BEGINNINGS

ARE YOU READY TO EVANGELIZE

The Lord your God is moving all over the world. The winds of my Spirit are moving over the face of the earth. The fire of my Spirit is moving, is purging, is bringing into existence a bride, a glorified bride, a bride of radiance. Yes, as my Spirit is moving, he is beginning to fulfill that which was prophesied years ago. The winds, the fire, the purging are bringing in a great harvest of souls.

As you look out unto the fields of the world, you will see that they are ripe and ready to harvest. My Spirit has been preparing many for this time. As you go forth with my words of power and deliverance to the lost, a great harvest will take place. Many souls are ready to receive me as Savior and Lord. They are ready! They are ready! They are ready!

Go forth! Go forth! Go forth! Evangelize! Evangelize! Evangelize! My Spirit has already prepared the way for you. Reach out to the lost and they will be won to me.

> *Do you not say, 'Four months more and then the harvest'? I tell you, open your eyes and look at the fields! They are ripe for harvest.*   John 4:35

OBEDIENCE

DO YOU COMMUNICATE WITH YOUR WIFE

Your wife is called alongside of you to be a help-mate, to be a stabilizer in times of discouragement, a hope when you feel all is gone and when you ask the question, "What am I doing here?" She will help meet your deepest hurts and desires, if you let her.

Share your feelings more openly with her. Talk with her. She has changed by my Spirit from old habits and old ways. Yes, she is my vessel too, called alongside to help minister to you and to set you free.

Take her hand and hold it. Love her more and more. She is very special in my eyes. The tears that she does shed are like dew in the morning to me, and like the fresh rain upon the grass. You are one with her and you are to minister as one.

Hold on my son, Hold on. My path will be there for you to see. You will walk on it and love Jesus.

> *Husband, in the same way be considerate as you live with your wives, and treat them with respect as the weaker partner and as heirs with you of the gracious gift of life, so that nothing will hinder your prayers.* I Peter 3:7

ONENESS

ARE YOU WAITING ON GOD

Remember not the former things. Behold, I am doing a new thing. There is a new life and a new way for you. I am a God who does abundantly above all that you ask for or think about. The former things are gone and the new things are here.

Wait for me and hear my voice and I will show you what to do. Wait on me and I will answer your deepest need. Devastation has fled from your home. Will you question me as to my timing in your life? My time table is different than yours. Have you ever lacked anything my child? Have you truly ever had a need that I did not meet? I know the wait is hard and is difficult for you, but I am working and I am moving in your life. I am preparing in ways you do not know of.

Be at peace my child and fret not. A fresh anointing, a fresh spring, a fresh gusher is about to burst upon you. You will rise with life, hope and victory for your situation.

I have seen your steadfastness against great odds and I am very pleased with you. I am a God who loves, delivers and raises up to new responsibilities. The training is difficult, but as soldiers are trained, so I train you.

I am a lover to those who love me. I am a Father to the fatherless. I am a Shepherd, a gentle breeze and a mighty wind. Trust me my child. Trust me and walk in love. My Agape love will flow through you, my life, and my Spirit. Others will be delivered and set free.

Find rest, O my soul, in God alone; my hope comes from him. He alone is my rock and my salvation; he is my fortress, I will not be shaken. My Salvation and my honor depend on God' he is my mighty rock, my refuge. Trust in him at all times, O people; pour out your hearts to him for God is our refuge. Selah Psalms 62:5-7

PATIENCE

ARE YOU STRUGGLING WITH SIN

T ake off the weight and the sin that does easily tempt you and run with patience the race that is set before you. Run and do not look back. Keep your eyes on me and a new birth of position, power and anointing in me will take place.

Run and do not look to the left or to the right. I give abundant grace, mercy and revelation in all things. Shed, strip off the old man with its lusts and desires. Do not yield yourself as an instrument of unrighteousness, but yield to me that my glory will be realized in your life.

> *Therefore, since we are surrounded by such a great cloud of witnesses, let us throw off everything that hinders and the sin that so easily entangles, and let us run with perseverance the race marked out for us. Let us fix our eyes on Jesus, the author and perfecter of our faith, who for the joy set before him endured the cross, scorning its shame; and sat down at the right hand of the throne of God. Consider him who endured such opposition from sinful men, so that you will not grow weary and lose heart.* Hebrews 12:1-3

PERSEVERANCE

IS GOD GIVING YOU HIS BUILDING BLUEPRINT

U nless the Lord builds the house, those that labor, labor in vain. Unless the Lord builds the tower, those that labor, labor in vain. For unless I build the structure, it will fall, it will be in ruin. Yes, I am moving over the face of the earth looking for those who are willing to move by what I say. I am looking for those who will build my kingdom according to my plans and my design. For the plans of the mind are futile, are useless. The plans of my Spirit are dynamic, are strong and are firm. Unless the foundations are laid by me, the structure will topple, and will fall. I have a special plan, a specific drawing to be followed. As you seek me with your whole heart, not holding back, I will bless and I will reveal that plan to you. My plan is mighty. My plan is sure. My plan is strong.

I have called you into position in my army. I have called you to stand strong, firm and lead. Yes, I will pour out my Spirit upon you and yours and you will flow with a greater anointing, a greater urgency, and a greater unction. It is my Spirit that stirs you even now. It is my love poured out upon you that you are sensing within. As I move upon you, you will go forth with my power and my victory.

I have seen your tears, your fasting, your intercessions, your feelings of despair. I have brought you up out of many pits. I have put a new song in your heart and now you are ready to share what I give to you. You will speak forth what I say. You will walk humbly before me. As I move upon you, I will build my work for my honor and my glory.

I am returning soon and I am coming for a glorious bride; a bride of praise; a bride that is chaste; a bride that is holy and spotless. Walk hand in hand with me as a bride to a husband. Clasp my hand firmly. Look to me in all things. Love me with all your heart, for I have chosen you to bring my words to many.

> *Unless the Lord builds the house, its builders labor in vain. Unless the Lord watches over the city, the watchmen stand guard in vain.*
>
> Psalm 127:1

PLANS

DOES THE LAND BELONG TO YOU

I see your desires. I see your hopes. I see your aspirations to serve me with all of your being. I see your dreams. I see your willing heart to be a useable vessel of mine, fit for my use in the things I purpose and I designate. Yes, my child, I see all of these things and I am aware of each step of your life.

I know you have been through trials, through woes, through difficulties and it is I the Lord who has given you the victory and brought you through the sea to dry ground. It is I who gives you the victory even now, for no weapon formed against my people who are walking in my covenant, and in my blessings, will prosper.

Love your neighbor with all of your heart. As you would love me, love them. I the Lord give the victory over the enemy through steadfastness of purpose and singleness of mind to serve me no matter what the cost. Yes, I Am that I Am, in complete control of your situation.

Vindication comes from my hand. My weapons are not on the natural level, but are spiritual. They break down the strongholds that rise against you even now in the darkest hours. Satan is a liar, the father of lies. I am the way, the truth and the light of the world. That light will rise in you and victory will come.

Do not be slack, but stand upon my word and my promises. Hold to them. As I healed you once before, even now I am healing your spirit to believe me for the impossible. For I work through faith, through love and through my Spirit. Walk in faith. The enemy will not prevail against you as my standard, my word, is raised in positive confession.

Pray! Intercede! Bring my promises before me. What I give as blessing, no man will put asunder. As I gave the Israelite descendants the Promised Land, so I give to you and do not take back. The territory is yours. Walk up and down the land. Walk and pray. Walk in the name of Jesus saith the Spirit of hope.

> *The Lord said to Abram after Lot had parted from him, "Lift up your eyes from where you are and look north and south, east and west. All the land that you see I will give to you and your offspring forever. I will make your offspring like the dust of the earth, so that if anyone could count the dust, then your offspring could be counted. Go, walk through the length and breadth of the land, for I am giving it to you.* Genesis 13:14-17

POSSESSION

ARE YOU AN INTERCESSOR

T he winds of my Spirit are moving over the whole face of the earth. The breeze of my love and anointing are moving upon the hearts of my servants. The fresh balm of my healing virtue is quickening my body and becoming Zoe (life) to their flesh. Yes, I am moving, convicting of sin, drawing all men to me, giving them a chance, a last opportunity for many to receive my grace into their lives.

I am moving and calling for my body to be a body of praise unto my name. I am moving and calling forth intercessors to pray for people everywhere. I am drawing all men unto me.

Bring the lost in. Speak to them when you sit down, when you rise up, in the highways and in the byways. I am ready to return, to bring in the grain, the harvest into the barn, before the greatest out-pour of my wrath falls upon unregenerate man. They will cry out for rocks and mountains to fall upon them to take their very breath away, for great will be the devastation on mankind that death to them will be a pleasure. But, for many, death will not come.

My children, listen to my Spirit more carefully. When he says speak a word, speak it, for I prepare the way. I prepare those who are ready to receive my words of love and encouragement. Others will be saved because of your obedience and no blood will be laid to your charge. Yes, my child, I am serious,

serious, serious. I know that my return is soon. It is drawing nigh, nigh, nigh.

Listen to my voice. Be steadfast in the tasks I have chosen for you. Do not move from my perfect will in your life. Satan seeks to drive by force my sheep into wolves' territory where they become all cut and bruised. Then I have to draw back and heal. So much time is wasted.

I have called my people and am calling right now to redeem the time. Buy back the hours and years not spent in prayer for my kingdom. Buy it back with the weapons of warfare and begin today to commit yourself to praying for my people. Begin today. Begin today.

I will bless you in your goings out and coming in. Your church will leap, will grow, will abound in miracles for my kingdom. What is not will be brought into reality. What you do not see, will rise and stand before you. Yes, a price will have to be paid, for some of you will have to rise before dawn as I did when I walked on earth. But, if you will obey, I will give you new strength and a stamina that you have never known before.

The hour is nigh. I am returning for my bride. I love you. I love you. I love you. Did not I pay the price and shed my blood for you? Give me your all in total commitment and I will raise you to new heights of glory beyond your imagination. Your bondages will be broken. Your chains fall off. Your prison doors opened and I will lead you to the streets of glory.

During the days of Jesus' life on earth, he offered up prayers and petitions with loud cries and tears to the one who could save him from death, and he was heard because of his reverent submission. Although he was a son, he learned obedience from what he suffered. Hebrews 5:7-8

PRAYER

SON-IS GOD PREPARING YOU

I am moving. I am moving. I am moving. Even now I am preparing you to move into new areas of ministry. Yes, my Spirit is moving on the hearts of a people especially chosen by me for this time and for a purpose.

I know your sicknesses, your agony of soul, your anguish of heart. I know your feelings of insecurity and helplessness in your situation. But I am getting the scene ready for a move of my Spirit upon your life and family.

I prepare. I prepare. I prepare before giving responsibility. I prepare not in the way of man's knowledge, but in the way of my plans and my purposes. Put aside your fears. They do not come from me. I Am that I Am, a God of infinite understanding and compassion. The past is wiped away. I do not see it anymore. Picture yourself as I do, clean, pure, holy, ready for me to do a new thing in your life, ready to climb a new mountain of venture, ready to embark on a new course.

My son, I love you as a son. I love you as a brother. I love you as my bride. I search the hearts of men for willing vessels who will follow me unreservedly, no matter what the personal cost. I am looking for men who will leave all behind to run a course that is forward and unhindered by the past.

Take my word. Use it as a sword and shield against the darts of the evil one. Did not Satan flee with one simple command by me, "Get thee behind me for thus it is written?"

I know your faithfulness, your love and your desires. All will be satisfied in me. Your steps are ordered by me. I am coming soon. Theology, doctrine, word studies, paragraphs, thoughts are all useless unless guided by my infinite hand, my infinite knowledge, my infinite Spirit. Can anyone truly say that they know me? My ways are past finding out unless guided by my Spirit. I dwell in the reality, of no time, no space, pure infiniteness. I dwell where I cannot be found by man's thoughts. But I move, I speak, I whisper, a word here and there to the spirit where I dwell in fullness, in entirety.

I will speak to your spirit man. Listen carefully, lest you miss me, but I will speak again and again until the message is clear to you. I will never depart from my word. But my word will not always be understood at first. I will speak. I will speak. I will speak, by my word, by a witness, by an anointed leader and you will know the truth. It will set you free. You will know direction. It will set you free. You will know my name. It will set you free. You will know my covenant, my leading and my delivering hand.

> *However, as it is written: 'No eye has seen, no ear has heard, no mind has conceived what God has prepared for those who love him.' But God has revealed it to us by his Spirit.* I Corinthians 2:9-10

PREPARATION

IS GOD'S WORD IMPORTANT TO YOU

My peace I leave with you. My peace I give unto you. Let not your heart be troubled, do not let it be afraid. For I will answer you at the acceptable time. I will deliver you. I will set you free. Pain will be no more.

Walk in faith. Walk in love. Walk in my word. I, Jesus, want to do a great thing through you. Stand on my word. Confess it. Hold it in your heart. Memorize it. Let your mind be renewed with great passages of my word. For it will flow from your spirit like a pipe ready to burst forth with clear, cool water. My word will set you free. You will flow in a new way, a unique way with my spirit and my gifts. Do not look to the ministry of another. Do not look to those around you for approval. Step out in faith, believing my word. I will answer you.

When your words came, I ate them; they were my
joy and my heart's delight, for I bear your name,
O Lord God Almighty.   Jeremiah 15:16

PRIORITIES

IS ALL LOST

D o not fret. Do not fear. I am with you. I will never leave you or forsake you. Though you are in the midst of pain, I am there. Though all seems lost, I am there. Though trials and troubles seem long, I am there. Though difficulties seem to abound, I am with you.

Take my hand. Grasp it firmly. I am holding yours tight. I will never, no never, no never leave you in the mire. I will never, no never, no never forsake you. I will draw you up from your pit of seemingly destruction. I will put a new song in your heart. This song will come from your innermost being. It will be a song that will set you free. I love you. Be still and know that I am God.

> *When you pass through the waters, I will be with you; and when you pass through the rivers, they will not sweep over you. When you walk through the fire, you will not be burned; the flames will not set you ablaze. For I am the Lord, your God, the Holy One of Israel, your Savior.*
>
> Isaiah 43:2-3A

PROMISES

ARE YOU CALLED TO SPEAK TO CROWDS

As you have been faithful to me, so I am and will continue to be faithful to you. I will go with you. I will speak to you. I will give you new hope and new direction. I will minister to you in a special way. As my Spirit has called you out, so my Spirit is calling you now. You are in a time of rest, a time of refreshing, a time of seriousness, of soul searching. As I raised up my vessels of old and trained them at great lengths, so I am raising you up. The training is hard and is extensive. For I equip my vessels for great tasks for my glory. I equip them and send them out.

I will set a new task before you, a task of efficiency and of great magnitude, for my Spirit is moving you forward and out. My Spirit is moving you in a more perfected path, a path of deliverance to many. You will speak my words of deliverance to one here, one there, to great crowds and to different flocks. I am calling you forth on a multi-level path, but a path that is strong, firm and sure. It is a surprise to you, different, one that is unexpected by you. But unfolding before you is my plan. Walk before me in humility. Walk before me in my strength.

> *Jesus went through all the towns and villages, teaching in their synagogues, preaching the good news of the kingdom and healing every disease and sickness. When he saw the crowds, he had compassion on them, because they were harassed and helpless, like sheep without a shepherd. Then he said to his disciples, 'The harvest*

*is plentiful but the workers are few. Ask the Lord
of the harvest, therefore to send out workers into
his harvest field.'*   Matthew 9:35-38

PROMOTION

DOES YOUR MINISTRY NEED MONEY

A m I not a mighty God who sees his children? Am I not a mighty God who grants visions and plans? Am I not a mighty God who gives the best presents, in my time and in my way? Do not fret because of those who prosper in the way, yet do not give to my work. Am I not mightier than those who are disobedient to me? Am I not mightier than those who do not give out of the abundance of their possessions?

I am not moved by disobedience. I am not moved by lack of faith. I am not moved by situations in my body. I am a mighty God, above all those things. Yes, even as I said, I will supply. Yes, I will do what I say. I will supply in ways that have not entered your mind or your spirit. For my ways are not your ways, nor my thoughts your thoughts. I will supply each and every need. I will do abundantly above all that you ask or think. And when you look back on the road which I have chosen, you will know that it is the Lord your God that has led you.

Rise! Take courage! My Spirit will stir my people. The finances will come in, in unexpected ways and by unexpected resources. You will know that my ideas, my thoughts and my plans prosper.

Rise! Have hope! A vision is to be fulfilled and yes, already has been.

The Lord will grant you abundant prosperity—
in the fruit of your womb, the young of your

livestock and the crops of your ground—in the land he swore to your forefathers to give you. The Lord will open the heavens, the storehouse of his bounty to send rain on your land in season and to bless all the work of your hands. You will lend to many nations but will borrow from none.

Deuteronomy 28:11-12

PROVISIONS

DO YOU FEEL UNQUALIFIED TO LEAD

There are times in my kingdom that are different from the times of men. There are places in my kingdom, seats, thrones that are different from the authorities of men. There are leaders in my kingdom that men would say, "Oh, that person does not have knowledge to be a leader." But know this, my ways are different than man's ways. My understanding's past finding out in the natural realm.

As I move upon you in the days ahead, man will say, "What are you doing in that place of leadership?" But know this, my child, I have called you. I have prepared you. I have led you to a new path, a path ordained by my Spirit. In the natural realm, it is different to you, but in my Spirit, it is perfect. Walk on that path. Be obedient and I will bless you. I will give to you the thoughts necessary to complete the chosen task. Let your mind be renewed in my word and learn from my anointed leaders. You will go forth in power, in victory and in hope to lead my people.

> *So he (Jesse) sent and had him (David) brought in.*
> *He was ruddy, with a fine appearance and hand-*
> *some features. Then the Lord said, 'Rise and anoint*
> *him; he is the one.' So Samuel took the horn of oil*
> *and anointed him in the presence of his brothers,*
> *and from that day on the Spirit of the Lord came*
> *upon David in power.*   I Samuel 16:12-13

QUALIFICATIONS

ARE YOU REACHING OUT TO YOUR BROTHERS

D id I not say to you that I would deliver you; I would move upon you; I would set you free? Know this, my child, nothing delights me more than praise unto my name. Nothing moves me more than intercessory prayer. Nothing thrills me more than an obedient heart in all things.

If my people who are called by my name would just begin to reach up to me in obedience and praise, and reach out to their Christian brothers, I would open up the heavens for them and shower down unlimited blessings that have not entered their minds or hearts. Some of these blessings are prosperity, health, and more than the natural, blessings of love, joy and peace. The unsaved souls of men will witness this unity and be won to me because you loved one another.

Pray my child. Yes, pray my children. The clock is just about ready to strike twelve. The midnight hour is almost here. Look up to the sky, your redemption is nigh. It is closer than any of you think it is. The dark hours are approaching soon upon the earth. My threshing floor is almost ready. The harvest is here. My sickle is prepared for a time on the earth that man has never known, nor will they know again.

Reach up in praise my children. My whole Deity is moved by it. Reach out my children. The Lord your God returns soon to set up his kingdom. Follow me! Follow me! Follow me! I will make you fishers of men.

*I have given them the glory that you gave me,
that they may be one as we are one: I in them and
you in me. May they be brought to complete unity
to let the world know that you sent me and have
loved them even as you have loved me." "Do not
say, 'Four months more and then the harvest'?
I tell you, open your eyes and look at the fields!
They are ripe for harvest.*   John 17:22-23 &
John 4:35-36

REACHING OUT

ARE YOU PULLING BACK

I f my people who are called by my name will humble them-selves and pray, I will heal the land. If my people who are called by my name will humble themselves and seek me with their whole heart, I will forgive their sins. I will pour out a blessing. I will make the crooked places straight. If my people who are called by my name will crucify the godless deeds of the flesh and give up what is not of me, I will pour out a mighty move of my Spirit across the land. Yes, I am moving swiftly over the face of the earth to bring into subjection my body, my people. For when my people are in submission to me and my word, I can move by my Spirit without hindrances, without interruptions.

My return is soon. My Spirit is moving in my body. Many of you are hearing my servants speak in boldness, in authority, in might and in power. Many of you are surrendering to my anointed word, but many of you are pulling back. Yes, do not pull back and harden your hearts in unbelief, but surrender all to me so I can purge, cleanse and bless. I am a God of love, of mercy and of compassion.

I know your needs. Am I not a God capable of supplying the largest things? Am I not a God who sees the smallest item? Nothing is too small, or too large, for me to answer. I will move through each need without respect of persons. I love you my people and as you seek me in all things, I will bless.

> *For in just a very little while, He who is coming will come and will not delay. But my righteous one will live by faith. And if he shrinks back, I will not be pleased with him.*　　　　Hebrews 10:37-38

RESISTANCE

ARE YOU ASKED TO CALL THE PRAYING WOMEN

Y ou are beautiful in my eyes, a flower on a tree, and a blossom of sweet fragrance. I have been moving upon you in a new way. I have been giving you my strength and my power to bring forth my glory to many people.

I will be visiting you in a special way. I will be creating within you new and special thoughts. You will wonder where these thoughts came from, but know this my child, they came from me, from my Spirit. There will be ideas that will be new, fresh and alive. These ideas will cause my work in you to prosper, to grow, to multiply and multiply again.

I have seen your humble and contrite heart. I have seen your tears of love and compassion for others. I have seen your tears of intercession and faithfulness to my work. I am moved and I am pleased with you. Though numbers may vary, yet I am with you and my Spirit rests upon you. Men in the government cabinet are being set free. Women are returning to their husbands, children are leaping for joy in my presence. You do not see this with the natural eyes, but my Spirit does. My Spirit moves through the barricades of darkness as you intercede on behalf of others.

A great wave of my Spirit will come upon you to intercede for the nation. Be obedient. Call the weeping and wailing women together, by twos, by threes and by many. A great breakthrough will take place. There will be a move of grace, a move of Godly sorrow and weeping, a move of compassion and love for the lost, for your country. I love you. Look up for your redemption draws nigh.

> *This is what the Lord Almighty says: 'Consider now! Call for the wailing women to come; send for the most skillful of them. Let them come quickly and wail over us till our eyes overflow with tears and water streams from our eyelids.'*
>
> Jeremiah 9:17-18

RESPONSE

HAVE YOU BEEN SACRIFICIALLY PRAISING ME

T he other day I opened a big package and in it were all kinds of surprises from you. There were notes of praise and a new song sung unto me. There were letters of joy and a sacrifice of thanksgiving to me when you were depressed, all alone and felt rejected. Know this my child, such surprises please me. They make me happy. They release me to give back to you all that you need.

I love you and want to do what is best for you and for my whole body. But so many times I am bound by pettiness, and party spirits. I want all of my body to release themselves in praise unto my name so that I can come back for a joyful, happy bride, dipped in my blood and released unto me as an offering to my Father.

I am coming soon. So many of you are not aware of this. You go buy and sell and act as though nothing will ever happen. But I am coming back and I have so many surprises for all of you. I have great big packages, unopened, waiting just for you.

Be patient in trials and tribulations. I know your heart and I know your desires. Sing praises unto me. Pray and let those prayers come unto me in faith, believing my Word.

Offer a sacrifice of a contrite and broken heart unto me. Let my sweet Spirit unite your heart in oneness with me. Freedom is yours for the taking. Bondage is already gone. Walk where my path and light goes, no one else's. Try the spirits to see if they are of me and walk in liberty, walk in liberty, walk in liberty. I have delivered you out of Egypt, out of the house of bondage. I love you and I welcome your sacrifice of praise unto my name, saith the Spirit of Hope.

> *Sacrifice thank offerings to God, fulfill your vows to the Most High, and call upon me in the day of trouble; I will deliver you and you will honor me.* Psalm 50:14-15

SACRIFICE

DO YOU WANT TO KNOW GOD BETTER

L earn of me! Learn of me and the spiritual hunger you have for a greater knowledge of me will be fulfilled. I have seen your heart and your spirit. I look into the depths of the innermost being. Your desire to know me and be loved by me, in a greater way, will be fulfilled.

I will come to you. I will visit you, through knowing my word, through a thought, through an impression. You will know it is me for it will be life unto your soul.

Seek first my kingdom in all things. Seek for me as you would a hidden treasure and you will find me. Study my word. Hide it in your heart. Speak my word with full authority, for the talents I have placed within you shall come forth in a greater anointing as my word is proclaimed through you. I have chosen you. I love you.

> *Oh, the depth of the riches of the wisdom and knowledge of God! How unsearchable his judgments, and his paths beyond tracing out!*
>
> Romans 11:33

SEEKING

HAVE YOU TROUBLE SPEAKING

I am a God of strength. I am a God of direction. I am God, El Shaddai, the all sufficient one. I am all these things and more to you. Why are you concerned? Why are you cast down in spirit? It is I who choose to flow through you. It is I who choose the way you should speak. It is I the Lord who blots out what is not of me. And what is of my word will never return void.

Others will not always understand my leading in your life. Others will criticize. But I the Lord accept you, love you and minister to you. In the days ahead I will reveal unto you deeper revelation knowledge and you will minister my word under a fresh and new anointing. Others will know it is my word flowing forth from anointed power. A new hunger for my word will arise within you and you will know it comes from my Spirit. The past is over. It is gone. New horizons are ahead.

I do not look for perfection, but for a willing vessel who wants to be used by me. My glory and my Spirit rest upon you. My words will come forth not in man's wisdom, but in a demonstration of the Holy Spirit and power.

Walk in faith. Walk in my word. Walk in hope, for my blood washes all away. My burdens are easy. My yolk is light. My calling is sure and mighty. I am a God of great variety and movement in my body. I raise up one with a word of faith. I raise up another with a word of hope. I raise up another with a word of might, a word of courage. Go forward as a soldier with full armor on. Do not let the enemy distract you. Stand firm against him for he seeks to devour. Praise me. Praise me. I dwell in praise and worship. I dwell between the wings of the cherubim. I dwell within you. I Am that I AM, a God pleased with you.

My message and my preaching were not with wise and persuasive words, but with a demonstration of the Spirit's power, so that your faith might not rest on men's wisdom, but on God's power. I Corinthians 2:4-5

SPEAKING

ARE YOU IN PAIN

I am the Lord your God that loves you. I am the Lord your God that delivers. I am the Lord your God that sets free from all bondage, all evil, all injustice. When you were but a little one, I knew you and picked you out to bring my word of hope and salvation to many. It was the Lord your God who equipped you to minister unto my name before many. It was I who said, "There is one who will obey me."

I have seen your faithfulness unto me and I am moved. I have seen your love for me and I am pleased. I have seen your times of distress. I have seen your tears. I have seen you when you walked all alone and felt lonely, discouraged and depressed. But my child, I have always been there with you. Even now I hold your hand through these days of seemingly devastation and destruction.

Take courage! Take heart! I am with you, with you, with you. I will never, never, never let you go. I will uphold you, strengthen you, be there all the time no matter where you may be. My Shekinah glory is with you in all your ways.

I love you my child. I love you my child. I love you. I need your praise unto my name, for Satan cannot dwell in the midst of praise and holiness.

I know your pain, but I will not leave you in the bed of seemingly destruction. I will raise you up to new heights of glory. My

Word will never, no never, no never return void. It will accomplish what I want it to.

You have been obedient and faithful in all places where I have sent you. I will bless, bless, bless you beyond anything you can imagine with your mind. My ways are not your ways, my thoughts not your thoughts. I deliver all my righteous ones from oppression. I deliver all who call upon my name. The prison doors are already open. Walk through that door and let my sweet Spirit set you free. You are my bride, my love, my praise. Eyes have not seen, nor ears have heard, nor has it entered into your mind, all I still have for you to do. You have been faithful in little things; I can now put you over much. I am Jehovah, Rophe.

> *So do not fear, for I am with you; do not be dismayed, for I am you God. I will strengthen you and help you; I will uphold you with my righteous right hand.*   Isaiah 41:10

SUFFERING

HAVE YOU BEEN A FAITHFUL WRITER

I t is the Lord your God that has begun this work in you. My life, my Spirit, my work, my words will pour out of you like water through a pipe. You are my chosen vessel. Have not I delivered you from all things? Is anything too hard for me to do? No task is impossible when I have an obedient, useable vessel. All my promises are true. They are purified, seven times, ground into the ground and blossom forth like a tree in spring ready to bare the season's fruit.

I am raising you to greater tasks for my glory during these last days. When the enemy comes in like a flood, I will raise a standard against him, for my spirit is always moving to and fro searching the hearts of my children.

I am looking, looking, yes, I am calling out men, women, and children to be my vessels of prayer. An intercessory prayer ministry is set before many of you. I will call. I will call. I will call. Walk in faith believing. Stand upon my word. Speak it to me and I will honor it, for I cannot deny what is of me.

I am moving. I am moving. I am moving. Yes, in all corners of the earth my spirit is hovering. Do not fear what man may say. Not all of my children walk in faith. Listen for my voice and my voice alone. It will be a whisper, a thought, a word, confirmed by two, by three and by my Word.

You have been faithful. Your hand has been my hand, your pen, my pen. I am moving in you in a greater way to flow in eloquence and simplicity, so all my children can understand me better. Be obedient to the call I have upon you to write. Do not shrink back in fear and unbelief. Nothing is impossible with God. Go forward and the sea will part. You will walk on dry land. The wilderness might seem long, but my anointed leading will bring you into the greatest fruit you have even known.

I love you my child. I love you my child. I love you my child. My peace is with you and you will just know, that you know, that you know I am moving and I am leading. Let the glory of my countenance light the way. Praise me. Praise me. Praise me. I am Jehovah Shammah. I am present wherever you go.

> *When the Lord finished speaking to Moses on Mount Sinai, he gave him the two tablets of stone inscribed by the finger of God.*
> Exodus 30:18

TALENT-WRITING

DO YOU HAVE TROUBLE CONTROLLING
YOUR TONGUE

I am the Lord! There is no one else. I am the Lord! There is no one else. I Am The Lord! Walk before me and be thou perfect, be thou holy.

Do not reveal secrets with your tongue, for Satan would seek to ensnare you; he would seek to enslave you. As you keep confidences, I will bless you more and more with the ministry of intercession. I have many secrets to share with you, but you are not yet ready. But as you let me help you curb your tongue, making it obedient to my word, I will bless.

Do not be discouraged, my child, but yield your tongue to me in all things. Listen for my voice before you speak and you will know what you are to share with others and what you are to keep secret.

I am Holy! I am coming back for a glorious bride without spot and wrinkle. Let me cleanse you now by my word. I am preparing you for many things. Your tongue will be a tongue of an exhorter. Your tongue will speak my words. Your tongue will flow with love and compassion and I will cleanse you of all idleness, backbiting and gossip. Your tongue will be pure before me in all things and you will speak my words of power and deliverance.

> *We all stumble in many ways. If anyone is never at fault in what he says, he is a perfect man, able to keep his whole body in check.*   James 3:2

TEMPERANCE

ARE YOU A MAN-CALLED OF GOD

I know of your heart's desire. I know of your desire not to make a mistake in discerning my leading in your life. I know of your feelings of inadequacy. I know of your joy, your anxieties and your frustrations. I know of the mantle that I have placed upon your shoulders. For it is I the Lord that has placed it there and no man shall take it from you. No women shall infringe upon it. No person shall have it. For when I lead, I lead all the way. And when I go before and light up dark corners, I light up all the way. Even the darkest night is as light when my glorious presence is there.

I know what lies ahead and I shall light up what is not seen by you at this time. I shall make plain to you what is not of my leading. My word and my shield shall go before you in all things. My word of victory and my word of power shall be your guide and protection. I will go before you as a Shepherd goes before his flock and you will know, that you know, that you know, that this is the way, walk in it.

I know of your desire like that of Moses of old, not to go forward unless I am with you. Be it known unto you my son, I was with you even in the womb. I called you out amongst young men to walk with me and to put me first in all things. As my Spirit drew you, you did put me first in all things. The years of not being productive are all gone. The years of fruitfulness for my kingdom are here. In the months ahead you will sense a greater anointing for the exploits ahead of you. You will speak forth with great boldness to those around you the Word of the Lord. As you lay prostrate before me, circumcised in heart, I will reveal myself to you. I have seen your faithfulness and I am pleased. I have seen your love for me and I am pleased. I will provide and I will meet every need. I will do abundantly above all that you can imagine. I am a God of new beginnings and great exploits. I am Jehovah Rophe, the Lord that heals you.

> *A shoot will come up from the stump of Jesse; from his roots a Branch will bear fruit. The Spirit of the Lord will rest on him—the Spirit of wisdom and of understanding, the Spirit of counsel and of power, the Spirit of knowledge and of the fear of the Lord.* Isaiah 11:1-2

TENDER SHOOT

ARE YOU TIMID

The God of all comfort is your strength. The God of all deliverance is your power. The God of all beauty is your hope even in the most impossible situation. As my Son surely rose out of the grave and conquered the powers of hell, so you will rise with new vigor and a new vision for the task that I have before you.

I have seen you lying upon your bed with your tears dropping on the pillow. I have seen you when you have sat in church and tears welled up in your eyes till you thought your heart would break. Yes, my child, I have seen your tears of compassion for souls and for my complacent body. For it is my Spirit that has moved upon you and I have flowed out of you through those tears. As surely as my Spirit moved you to cry in compassion, so my Spirit will move upon you to mount up with strong words of boldness for my Kingdom.

Stir up the gift I have placed within you and praise me, praise me, praise me. I will do a new thing within you if you will be obedient in all things. Timidity is nothing in my eyes for I give boldness of heart and speech as my servants ask for it in faith.

> *For God did not give us a spirit of timidity, but*
> *a spirit of power, love and of self-discipline.*
>
> II Timothy 1:7

TIMIDITY

ARE YOU BEARING A SPECIAL BURDEN

As my Spirit is moving over the face of the earth, I am calling forth mighty women of valor. As my Spirit is moving over the face of the earth, I am calling forth men who will hear my voice.

Yes, even as a child I knew you. I knew you and called you from the womb to be an anointed vessel of mine. Do not doubt the call I have on your life. Though clouds come and rain falls, does it not bring forth the harvest and the fruit in due season? Though you walk through storms, does not the storm have a starting time and an ending time? This thing that you are going through is of me. It is of my leading. Am I not a Shepherd? Am I not a father who chastens? Am I not one who prepares the way for my servants? I go before in all these things. I go before and prepare for great exploits. The training is hard. The training is not easy. The training is difficult. But as my Spirit leads, I anoint. As my Spirit teaches, I set free. Even now the burden you bear is part of the cross and is a part of my leading. But in the fullness of time, I will set you free. You will know that you know that the Shepherd has gone before, for my yolk is easy and my burden is light. I take the burden. I bear it in your place.

I see your heart. It is one of a servant. I see your desire to be all that I have wanted you to be and I am pleased. But let it be known unto you my child, your eyes have not yet seen what I have in store for you. As you follow me in all things, unfolding before you is a great plan, a plan you have not expected. As I prepare you, train you and lead you, you will be ready to put on this mantel and special leading. As I lead you out, you will look back and say, "Oh, this is why the training was so hard."

You are anointed by me to serve me with all of your heart, soul, and mind. As you serve me completely in all things, this three-fold cord will stand firm.

Rise my child. I have much work for you to do. I will open doors of ministry and you will see my hand in all things. Though others do not understand you, I do. Though they might scoff, I never will. Though they might say, "Oh another woman, another man", I say, "Oh another vessel of God; another one for me to use." And I will use you. Do you believe this?

> *As for God, his way is perfect; the word of the Lord is flawless. He is a shield for all who take refuge in him. For who is God besides the Lord? And who is the Rock except our God? It is God who arms me with strength and makes my way perfect.* Psalm 18:30-32

TRAINING

MOTHER, ARE YOU IN TRAVAIL

E ven as you have birthed your child in the flesh, so you are birthing him now in the Spirit. The travail is strong. The travail is mighty. The travail is hard and it is difficult.

I have seen your tears my dear one. I have seen your groaning. I have seen you weep upon the pillow when you have felt your heart would break. Yes, I have seen all of this. It has not gone unnoticed. I am moving. I am moving in a mighty way even now in answer to those prayers. Oh, it might seem as though nothing is happening, but as you have been praying, strongholds are being broken for my honor and for my glory. Continue! Continue! Continue! Pray, pray, pray as my Spirit continues to move upon you. A breakthrough is imminent.

Trust me in all things. Am I not God, capable of wrapping my arms around even the youngest of your children? Am I not God, capable of protecting them from harm? Yes, I am the best Father to them, the best Mother, the best Friend. Be encouraged, for the burden you bear shall be lifted by a mighty anointing of my Spirit. It shall come to pass! It shall come to pass! It shall come to pass! Be strong in my Spirit. That which is feeble, I will strengthen. That which is weak, I will make strong. I love you.

They will come with weeping; they will pray
as I bring them back. I will lead them beside
streams of water on a level path where they will

not stumble, because I am Israel's father, and
Ephraim is my firstborn son.   Jeremiah 31:9

TRAVAILING

HAS YOUR HUSBAND HURT YOU

Your husband has hurt you. His coarse words have wounded your spirit. But know this, my child, I heal all who come to me in faith believing. I heal and set free those locked in cages of fear, anxiety and trouble. It is the Lord that heals the deepest scars and deepest wounds. Jesus is my name, and in me is all life.

Trust me my child. Trust me as you would your own father. Let my sweet spirit set you free. Let my love pour forth out of you and you will be in liberty, liberty, liberty. Truly the bells will ring in your soul. Confess your innermost thoughts to me. Hide nothing from me for I see all and know all.

I love you and more than anything else, I want you to love me. Leave your man in my hands. Am I not capable of handling him, of wooing him, of bringing him to salvation's drinking water?

I know how Satan has tested you and tried you, till you even spared of life itself. But I have never left you, never forsaken you, and never let you go. Even when the waters almost swept over your head, I pulled you up. I set you on dry ground. Yes, I set you on mountain tops till the fresh air of heavenly places breathed new life into you. I the Lord have done this. Yes, even when your faith has been small, I have moved on your behalf.

Now, rise from your state of depression. Let my name and my word revive you. Hold on. Stay single of mind, with one purpose. Believe, believe, believe. Nothing is impossible with my Father. I will intercede for you as I have promised. I will fulfill my word and blessings unnumbered will pour forth to you and your household. I am the Lord of your home, of your situation. Believe it and be satisfied.

> *I waited patiently for the Lord; he turned to me and heard my cry. He lifted me out of the slimy pit, out of the mud and mire. He set my feet on a rock and gave me a place to stand. He put a new song in my mouth, a hymn of praise to our God. Many will see and fear and put their trust in the Lord.*   Psalms 40:1-3

TRUST

DO YOU FEEL GOD HAS FORGOTTEN YOU

A m I a God that forsakes his own? Am I a God to leave someone alone in the wilderness? Does not my word tell you that I will never leave you nor forsake you?

I see your need for healing. I see your need to be set free. I see your need for victory over all the circumstances of life. Am I not a God of power? Am I not a God of might? Am I not a healing God that makes whole body, soul and spirit? Yes, I am all these things and much more.

I am all-powerful and all-knowing. I am always present with you in all of your circumstances and trials in life. In all these things, I am still with you.

Though you feel alone, like no one understands and no one cares, yet I am a God that understands. I see your need for love. It will be met in me. I see your desire for ministry. It will be fulfilled in time.

I am getting ready to move in on your situation. It will be little by little. As I unfold my plans to you, you will see my hand moving and my hand that will lead you forward.

Let my Holy Spirit bury the past so that it will never rise again. Let my Holy Spirit put you on a new path for my honor and glory in your life. My power is before you, my fire behind you, and my love surrounds you.

Others will not always understand my leading in your life, but my love will protect you and my word will guide you. Prosperity is ahead of you.

You are entering a new phase of training. There will be spiritual forces to overcome. But as you raise high my banner of love, my banner of authority, my word of truth, Satan will flee and victory will be yours. Rise now my child. Take courage. A fresh new anointing is ready to fall upon you.

> *For I am convinced that neither death nor life,*
> *neither angels nor demons, neither the present*
> *nor the future, nor any powers, neither height*
> *nor depth, nor anything else in all creation, will*
> *be able to separate us from the love of God that*
> *is in Christ Jesus our Lord.*   Romans 8:38-39

UNDERSTANDING

DO YOU WANT TO SING

I know your desire to sing like a bird. I know your desire to soar like the eagle. I know your desire to be set free. I know your spirit. I know your feelings of, "I can't do it."

Know this, my child, (for I still see you as my child no matter how many earth years you are) know this, my anointing is upon you in a new and fresh way. My anointing will rise within your spirit to move you in new territories and new paths. Your feelings of inadequacy are all covered with my blood and my anointing.

Be faithful to me. Be faithful to me. Be faithful to me. He that is faithful and of a contrite heart in little things, I will restore and put over much. The years of the locust are past. The years of ministry are ahead.

Satan will try to discourage you, but don't listen to his voice. My voice is like a soft word here and a soft word there, which says, "This is the way, walk in it." My paths are paths of freedom, not bondage. My moving in your spirit is always one of love.

Learn to discern by my word, the moving of the soul nature and the moving of the Spirit of God. My word is always accurate and it is quick, sharp and powerful giving discernment into the things of God and the things of the evil one.

Your tears have flowed on many occasions. But they are all recorded. They are all written down in my book. I see them all, and I love you. Know this also, my child, I was rejected once too, but I went forward, by the Holy Spirit, and conquered. You will be rejected from time to time. But turn it over to me and I will heal, deliver and set free. I will take those rejections and turn them around to glorify me. Let your face reflect my image moving through you for it is not you who are singing, but my Spirit in you.

> *I can do everything through him who gives me strength.*   Philippians 4:13

> *Praise the Lord. Sing to the Lord a new song, his praise in the assembly of the saints.*Psalm 149:1

UNHINDERED

DO YOU NEED UNITY WITH YOUR SPOUSE

I am your Lord. I am your Savior. I will be supreme in your life and the life of your loved one. You are one, one, one in me and surely my anointing is upon the two of you. I, the Lord, have chosen you to be ministers unto me for my glory.

I have seen your faithfulness and I am pleased. I have seen your courage, and I am pleased. I have seen your fears and how you have fought Satan and have won, for you both know my name and my delivering power.

Trust me! Trust me! Trust me! Your children will rise with strength, power and leadership in the coming days.

I am coming soon and I am calling for men, women and children who will surrender all unto my name. I love you, saith the Spirit of the Lord, and I long for us truly to be in each other's presence in my Father's Kingdom. It will be soon! It will be soon! It will be soon! Occupy until I come back.

> *I will give them singleness of heart and action, so that they will always fear me for their own good and the good of their children after them.*
>
> Jeremiah 32:39

UNITY

ARE YOU IN THE HOLY OF HOLIES

The breakthrough is coming! Raise high my banner of love. Raise high my banner of correction. Raise high my banner of intercession. When I am lifted up, men will be drawn to me.

Praise me in the Holy of Holies. Some of you want to stay in the outer court where many wolves can get in and destroy, but as you enter into the Holy of Holies, the sweet incense of praise and intercession is coming up to my nostrils and your prayer and praise is wielded back to the earth upon all unbelief, upon all that is not of me. Nothing is too hard for me to do. As I parted the Red Sea and others walked on dry ground, so I can part your way and others can walk on dry ground also. As they see your hands lifted up in faith, so they will be strong and fight till the victory is won. Others will see my faith, my love and my strength through you. I love you.

> *You broaden the path beneath me, so that my ankles do not turn. I pursued my enemies and overtook them; I did not turn back till they were destroyed. I crushed them so that they could not rise; they fell beneath my feet. You armed me with strength for battle; you made my adversaries bow at my feet. You made my enemies turn their backs in flight and I destroyed my foes.*
>
> Psalms 18:36-40

VICTORY

IS SATAN BUFFETING YOUR HEALING MINISTRY

P ersecutions and harassments for the sake of the Gospel is your cross to bear daily. You are to pick up that cross, stand up for me and follow me. Some will die for my name's sake. Some will be stoned for my name's sake. Some will walk heavy paths of persecution to get my word out to the heathen. This is to be expected. If the prophets were persecuted, if I was persecuted, do you suppose that you will not be also?

Come now, let us reason together. My word is powerful. Even in persecution I can move by my word to protect, to hover, to guide out of distressful situations. I can move you even through crowds unnoticed. Even in the midst of persecution, I am able to deliver. But remember this, my child, not all will be. Some will be delivered up to councils, peoples, and Governments for my name's sake. Does this then mean that my word fails? My word becomes null and void? My word never fails. It never returns void. Even in death, there is victory. Even in death there is life. Even in persecution, there is hope.

Come now, let us reason together again. My life was give as a ransom for many. My life was given so you can be set free from the powers of darkness. My life was surrendered to the enemy so that you can be free from his dominion and power. I bore your sicknesses. Why do I need another sacrifice to bare sickness so that others will be saved? Wasn't my coming down from the glory of glories enough? Wasn't giving up my place in the heavenlies sufficient? Why do my men and women seek to reason this away when they do not see people healed? Do they want to reason away salvation too when others are not born again by my Spirit?

Let us reason further. When I gave myself as a sacrifice, perfect in body and spirit, my Father accepted it as atonement for all sin. My Father accepted it as a sweet smelling savor of obedience. My Father accepted it once and for all for the cleansing blood poured out on the Altar. Why do you need another to give up his life in sickness? I bore sickness. Do you think my Father is pleased with his people accepting sickness as coming from His hand for my glory to be realized in a situation?

Come now, let us reason again. Were not the stripes I bore enough? Did not the pain I go through satisfy redemption's plan? Why is my sacrifice made a desecration by my leaders when they see people leave this realm in sickness and say it was for my glory? Yes, even with the man born blind from birth, did not I heal him?

There is no glory in sickness. It does not come from my Kingdom. I bore sickness. I broke its power over my people. Accept that! Receive that!

Come now and we will reason again. You say, but I have fasted. I have stood on the word for that person and he died anyway. He died sick. He died in pain. My faith is down. It is all gone and I cannot believe anymore.

First of all my child, my word never changes. I bore sickness on the cross. I poured out my very life blood for your total well-being. Who do you suppose hinders that from being mani-fested? The person? Sometimes! Satan? Yes! For he still thinks he can deceive my people.

Am I a God who fails? Am I a God who forsakes? Am I a God who changes his redemption? So many of my people are perishing for lack of knowledge of my word.

Did not I pass on my authority to my Body? Did not I pass on my power of attorney in my name, in my sacrifice?

Why are my people perishing? Why do they lack this knowl-edge? Why do you pray, "Lord, if it be thy will, heal?" Yes, my child, it is my will to heal. You do not need to pray that. Why do you pray, "Lord you heal!" Have not I given you power over all the enemy? Take my authority. Even as you discipline your child and they obey because of who you are, so Satan needs to bow to my name in you for you are a part of my Body. Did not Moses stretch forth the rod in his hand, and the seas parted? I have given you a rod of power and victory. I have given you my anointing.

Am I not in you? Is not my image being formed in you? Even as you die daily to fleshly and carnal ways, so my Spirit, my Life comes alive, quickening what is not right to get in line with my word.

Oh my child, do not whimper. Do not cry. Do not shrink back in unbelief. Take my word. Tread down the works of darkness. Even in a natural battle, the enemy at times advances more. But yet as the pursuer goes forth in might, the battle is won. Do not let the defeats of others discourage you. Do not let sicknesses discourage you. Stand on my word. Preach it.

Proclaim it. Do not reason it away. Healing will take place. Others will be set free. My glory will be manifested. Even when my children die sick, they are set free from the dominion of darkness. Even if you do not understand, my glory can still go forth as you release that person to me.

> *I have given you authority to trample on snakes*
> *and scorpions and to overcome all the power of*
> *the enemy; nothing will harm you.* Luke 10:19

WARFARE

ARE YOU PRAYING THE WORD

My Children, love one another, for love is of God. As a new mother would care for her infant, so I want to care for you. As a Father would teach his son the ways of life, so I want to teach you the ways of my Spirit.

Be open my child to the ways of the Lord. Let my spirit have his way in your life. Do not quench him lest he be grieved. Discern his moving by my word. Anything opposite or contrary to my already written revelation is either of the soul nature and natural impulses or of the schemes and wiles of the evil one.

Get to know my word. Hide it in your heart. When my word abides in you like a hidden treasure in a cave, the evil one cannot penetrate for my word flows forth from hidden springs of the Spirit and quenches his darts.

The ways of an intercessor are hard and long. Much time needs to be spent by my body in prayer during these last days. I am calling out vessels willing to pay the price. I am calling out men, women and yes, even children to pray for needs as my Spirit prompts the regenerated spirit of man. Listen carefully for my voice, children. You might be one of those vessels. You will not need to look for any special path or special leading. You will just know, that you know, that you know that my voice is calling you into this vital ministry of intercession. Prayer and my word going forth in prayer, breaks the bonds of Satan. Don't you see why you must hide my word within your heart? As I move you in authoritative prayer, it then can flow forth like a gushing geyser. I have so many things prepared for my loved ones to see in my word; things that have not entered your heart, mind or even soul. I will be returning soon. I love you.

> *Take the helmet of salvation and the sword of the Spirit, which is the word of God. And pray in the Spirit on all occasions with all kinds of prayers and requests. With this in mind, be alert and always keep on praying for all the saints.*
>
> Ephesians 6:17-18

WEAPONS

DO YOU WANT TOMORROW TO BE SPECIAL

A s I have promised, so I will do. As I have promised, so I will act. Tomorrow will be a special day unto me; a day of thanksgiving, a day of praise, a day of testimony, and a day of joy. I have set this day apart for you to minister unto me. I need the fruit of your lips praising me and to know that my people love me.

I have given you much. Worship me in the beauty of holiness and I will deliver. I will set free. I will manifest myself in a special way. For my Spirit hovers. He moves in mysterious ways upon obedient servants of mine. As I move, I will be like a gentle breeze of Spring, like the fire of the blazing sun, like the sound of many rushing waters. I have seen your cry and I will answer. Worship me.

> *Through Jesus, therefore, let us continually offer to God a sacrifice of praise—the fruit of lips that confess his name.* Hebrews 13:15

WORSHIP

ARE YOU LIKE TIMOTHY

I have called you out like my servant Timothy of old. I have called you out among young men to flow with my Holy Spirit. The hunger that you have to know me shall be fulfilled. You will be equipped to carry my words to many.

Listen for my voice in all things. It will be a gentle whisper, a strong word, a word of hope through my anointed leaders. Submit to my anointed leaders and you will learn from them the Word of the Lord.

> *Study to shew thyself approved unto God, a workman that needeth not to be ashamed, rightly dividing the word of truth.* II Timothy 2:15 (KJV)

Speak my word. Hide my word in your heart and it shall flow out of you like a mighty river of life. I will enlighten your mind as you seek me in all things. You are mine. I have called you.

> *In the last days, God says, I will pour out my Spirit on all people. Your sons and daughters will prophesy, your young men will see visions, your old men will dream dreams. Even on my servants, both men and women, I will pour out my Spirit in those days, and they will prophesy.* Acts 2:17-19

YOUTHFUL

II. TO MY SHEPHERDS

Be shepherds of God's flock that is under your care, serving as overseers-not because you must, but because you are willing, as God wants you to be; not greedy for money, but eager to serve; not lording it over those entrusted to you, but being examples to the flock. And when the Chief Shepherd appears, you will receive the crown of glory that will never fade away.

I Peter 5:3-4 (NIV)

IS GOD CALLING YOUR CONGREGATION
TO PRAYER

What you are doing, you are doing well. You are calling my people to a greater exploit and a greater move of my Spirit. You have heard my voice and are obeying my Father. And, yes, I say, do not be surprised at the reaction of others. Do not be surprised if all do not enter, for not all of my servants want to enter into this area of surrender. But as you blow the trumpet, as you set yourself apart for this time, I will speak to you and you shall have your heart's desire. Yes, shepherd of my fold, I am calling you into deeper wells, deeper waters and deeper ways. Even though some shall abandon the ship, you are to hold on to the stern, you are to steer the rudder. I am the Captain, and my voice is to be obeyed in all things.

This is a time for the people to search their hearts and to call upon me. Set aside a day for corporate prayer, a day to assemble together, a day of contriteness. As the day is set aside, it will result in a great outpouring of freedom of praise. Prison doors will be opened, and the captives set free.

This is a day of revelation, a day of knowing the Father. The day of Jesus is here, the day of the Holy Spirit is here, now the day of the Father shall take place. We shall flow as a triune among the people and they shall be brought into the most Holy Place. They shall know my glory, my presence and when they do, they shall leave with such power and might that kingdoms will be brought down in my three-fold name. I shall rise and

139

I shall reign forever more. Worship me. Worship me. Discard what is old and what is worn out. Let the new wine flow in full power.

> *Blow the trumpet in Zion, declare a holy fast, call a sacred assembly. Gather the people, consecrate the assembly; bring together the elders, gather the children, those nursing at the breast. Let the bridegroom leave his room and the bride her chamber. Let the priests, who minister before the Lord, weep between the temple porch and the altar. Let them say, Spare your people, O Lord. Do not make your inheritance an object of scorn, a byword among the nations. Why should they say among the peoples, Where is their God?* Joel 2:15-17

ASSEMBLY

HAVE YOUR FUNDS AND HOME BEEN STOLEN

D o not be moved by what you see. Do not be moved by your circumstances. Surely as I called you out, I will bless. Surely as I have called you forth, I will bless. Surely as I have instructed you to move out by my Spirit, I will bless. I will bless your labor. I will bless your ministry. I will bless your people.

Some will come and some will go, nevertheless I will bless and I will bring back those who have gone astray. I will bring back into the fold those who have gone into wolves' territory. My body is unique and I am moving all over the world to bring forth a people of celebration, power and victory for my honor and glory. Surely as I have called you out, I will confirm my Word. New people will come in, new men, new women and new children.

I have heard your cry and your many intercessions and I will bless. My body will be one. A great outpouring of my Spirit is ready to take place all over the world; another wave, a three-fold wave of contriteness of heart, of repentance and of dedication. As my Spirit begins to woo, to bring all into subjection, my body will grow in splendor and in radiance.

A great move is imminent in your life. I have promised you a dwelling place. I will fulfill my Word. The funds that were stolen and the house that was taken shall be returned by my Spirit. They are yours. They are yours. Walk in faith, believe my Word. I will watch over all my Word to perform it, to do it, to bring it to pass.

> *As the rain and the snow come down from heaven, and do not return to it without watering the earth and making it bud and flourish, so that it yields seed for the sower and bread for the eater, so is my word that goes out from my mouth: It will not return to me empty, but will accomplish what I desire and achieve the purpose for which I sent it. You will go out in joy and be led forth in peace; the mountains and hills will burst into song before you, and the trees of the field will clap their hands.* Isaiah 55:10-12

BLESSINGS

IS YOUR CHURCH IN DIVISION

M y Spirit, yes, my deity is moving swiftly upon the face of the earth. My harvest is ready to be reaped, my angels ready to go forth. Weep my children and mourn for those who will not be gathered into the grainier house. Weep my children and mourn for the wave of destruction that will come upon the earth. Weep and mourn for the men, women and children who have not made a decision to receive me as Savior before my return. Weep and mourn for their salvation yet to come. Many will be called during those days. Many will still refuse, calling for mountains to fall on them. Weep, oh daughters. Weep, my sons. Let your complacency and laughter be turned to mourning for the children of men, for the children yet unborn.

A new commandment I give now. A new word to many of you who have grown cold and lukewarm in your zeal and love for me. Love the brethren. Love your children. Love your family. Love your neighbors. Love! Love! Love! Do not back bite one another, lest you be devoured by the schemes of the evil one. Put back in place what is out of joint and serve me with unfailing love. If my body continues to devour one another with hatred, pettiness and party spirits, my work is hindered.

Cleanse yourselves from defilement. Let my sweet dove heal your broken spirits. Have faith in God, my Father. He is your strength, your hope, your deliverance. I want to return for my glorious bride, without spot and wrinkle in a perverse generation. Get your eyes off one another and put them back on me so you may be salt on the earth once more, lights on a hill, water for a thirsty generation.

Come to me, my children. Walk with me. Hold my hand and I will set you free from what ails you. Let my sweet Spirit flow through you, reviving what is dead, filling with what is good. Seek me first and my kingdom and all things shall be added unto you.

When I talked with my disciples face to face, they often were like a bunch of eager young boys seeing who could be king on the mountain. And my body of believers is often like that today, competing for the moving of my Spirit within them; competing for outstanding ministries, competing for men's applause. And I understand this. But remember, my children, he who is to be the greatest in my kingdom, must come to me as a child, basking in my love and serving all whom I bring across his path. When you humble yourself, expecting nothing in return but the glory of my presence, then I am free to move with my Spirit.

Love me! Love me! If you don't appear to others to be of importance, know this, my kingdom and my exaltations are of a greater nature than earths. I will exalt in due season all those who are faithful to what I say.

My children, pray, pray, pray. When you pray for others, you set yourself free from bondage.

There has never been a time on earth when my body needed to be together as now. Do not divide over words, over semantics, over thoughts. Stay as one, love me with all of your heart, soul and mind. My children, I love you. Stay faithful to me. I am always faithful to you. I will be seeing you soon.

> *What causes fights and quarrels among you?*
> *Don't they come from your desires that battle*
> *within you? Humble yourselves before the Lord,*
> *and he will lift you up.*   James 4:1, & 10

DIVISIONS

IS YOUR CHURCH CALLED TO EVANGELISM

The Lord your God is doing a mighty work. The Lord your God is moving over the face of the earth with great winds of power. The Lord your God is moving over the face of the earth with the purging fires, the fires of evangelism.

As my Spirit is moving, I am calling this body into position, into order. I have brought you through many trials and many difficulties in the past. In the days ahead, I will bring you through the rivers of trial again. My Spirit is moving and I am calling out a great army, an army equipped with my sword and my deliverance. My Spirit is calling you out as a body of celebration and praise, a body of evangelism to go forth with my word.

Reach out my children with the word of praise and as I move upon you in various ways to accomplish my goals and my direction, you will sense within you a burning desire, a desire like that of Jeremiah of old. It will be great upon many of you. It will be mighty. You will go into the city streets and market places with my word of authority to the lost and dying.

> *Then the master told his servant, Go out to the roads and country lanes and make them come in, so that my house will be full.* Luke 14:23

EVANGELISM

IS YOUR FLOCK YOUNG

I know your desire to serve me with all of your heart. I know your love for me. Yes, you have been faithful. I know your needs, your inadequacies, your desires, hopes, dreams and visions. My anointing has settled upon you and you are walking by faith. My hand of protection is upon you in all things. My light and my glory light the way.

Be still and just know that I am God. I build. I plant. I pluck up. I deliver. I heal. I set free. It is I who does these things in my time and in my way. Rest in me and know that I Am that I Am. I Am the Almighty God, Sovereign and in control of your life and my work through you. Look to me in all things. I will move. I will move. I will move. Those around you in prison will be set free. Those sick, healed. Those in need, prosper. For it is I the Lord that is mighty in work and wonders.

Trust me. Trust me. Trust me. Signs always follow my word of truth and faith. My delivering hand moves in the glory of praise and union with me.

Preach my word with holy boldness and fervor. Do not shrink back in any doubt and unbelief. Go forward and the walls of deception will crumble. Speak my word. Speak my word. Speak my word.

Your flock is young in me. They are like little lambs amongst the ravaging wolves and lions. Lead them with the rod of correction and the staff of learning. Go before them and prepare the way, as I go before you and prepare the way. Love them. Love them. Love them. When they cry, do not scold. Pick them up in your arms, as I do you, and hold close to your breast. Give them hope, encouragement and love and they will rise with you to great heights of faith. Give them my milk and when I tell you, give them my meat. Both will come forth from you as I move upon you in a new and mighty way.

I have chosen you. I have anointed you. I have delivered you and set you free. I Am that I Am. Much ministry lies before you and the struggles you are experiencing now are preparing you for great responsibility. Do you not train your son in the same way? An electric saw is not given before a little saw. I love you the same way and what I am doing in your life now is to prepare you to handle the electric saw. Take courage, take heart. I will never leave you. I will never forsake you, never let you down. I will go before you in all things. Lead my sheep. Feed My sheep. Love my sheep.

> *To this you were called, because Christ suffered*
> *for you, leaving you an example that you should*
> *follow in his steps.*   I Peter 2:21

EXAMPLE

HAVE YOU BEEN WAITING FOR GOD'S BLESSING

I have brought you into a wide and a firm path. Others are already asking, "Does God work like this?" Know this, my child, no weapon formed against you will prosper. No tongue raised against you will stand. I am forming in and through you my ministry in this hour, this place and this time. People will come from the north, the south, the east and the west. They will come by 1's by 2's and by hundreds. The Lord your God has opened the door and is moving you in new places and new ways. They will say as they walk in the door, "God is truly in this place." They will see my glory, my power, my tongue, my voice. They will laugh, they will weep, they will be full of joy and wonder at the miracles I will do.

There will be those in wheel chairs, bound by Satan, who will go free. Those that are blind, will see. Those dead, come alive; for I am the Resurrection and the Life. My Spirit will move and my Spirit will perform miracles. Praise will resound to me as sweet incense to my throne.

I will bless you. I will bless you. I will bless you. The years of the falcon are gone. The years of the eagle are here. You will soar. You will be free. I will reward your faithfulness.

Your flock has been faithful to you and to me. I will bless them with a special blessing. They will serve me with new fervor, and they will be exalted by me in work responsibilities and deeds for my glory. I will bless them. I will bless them. I will bless them.

Serve me with unfailing love. Adore me. Take rest in me. I will give to you my son and my daughter, new hope, new strength, new faith, for the Lord your God upholds you in all things.

> *Great is his love towards us, and the faithfulness*
> *of the Lord endures forever. Praise the Lord.*

Psalms 117:2

FAITHFULNESS

HAVE YOU BEEN WRONGLY ACCUSED

I am the God of new beginnings. I am the Lord of new paths of righteousness. I am the Spirit that moves in mysterious ways to the natural mind, to the natural senses, to the natural man. I move in the realm of the Holy Spirit and speak to the spirit of man with a word here, a word there, through spoken leaders, prophets and my written Word. I move and I work with the man who wants to serve me in love, in contriteness of heart and in humility.

I the Lord will give you strength, love and grace at new cross roads of my leading. I move and I bring into existence the perfect will of my Father for you.

Do not fear the cross roads. Though all may be confusing to you now, my Spirit will direct you out of the confused natural senses to perfect peace. I have seen your many tears as they have filled your eyes. I have seen them flow and I have been right there with you, holding you and your loved one in the hollow of my hand, under my wings of shelter, and under my canopy of protection.

I will never let you down in the days ahead. For a time it might seem you are in a wilderness, yet I am moving and I am equipping you as my Spirit directs you. You have many hurts. You have a wounded spirit. As the scar healed on my pierced side, so it will heal in your heart. I the Lord heal and yes, my mercy is great to my children, even to those who doubt my name. I am a God of infinite love and patience to the children of men.

You have been accused by others. I have heard all of this. But vindication is mine and I will chasten heavily. When my children accuse wrongly my anointed servants, they have touched me and wounded me and my body. I will chasten and correct for they have walked out of the canopy of my protection into dangerous wolves' territory where my rod of reproof will bring back into the fold.

Your heart has been pure, only desiring to do my will and my bidding. You have spoken to my sheep words of exhortation, love, mercy and repentance. You have been faithful. Do not fear what lies ahead. Without faith, it is impossible to please me. I will part the water. I will have you walk on dry ground. I will drown the enemy before you.

I have many sheep. They are in various folds. Do not fear. Do not fear. Listen for my voice and I will go before you and prepare the way for a new venture. Leave the past to me, the present to me, the future to me, and even the moment to me. I will bring you into the greatest victories, greatest conquests, and greatest move of my Spirit that you have ever known. My Spirit has chosen you. You have chosen me. You have surrendered your all to be a shepherd of my sheep. My son, my daughter, I will never forsake you and I will meet each need.

I consider that our present sufferings are not
worth comparing with the glory that will be

revealed in us. And we know that in all things
God works for the good of those who love him,
who have been called according to his purpose.

Romans 8:18, 28

FALSE ACCUSATION

DO YOU NEED GREATER LOVE

I say unto you, Shepherds over my flocks, preach the Word. Strengthen what is feeble, and what is out of joint. Love, love, love my sheep. Even the weak ones need cuddling. Even the sick ones need healing. Even the strong ones need words of encouragement. As you love my sheep, you love me. As you teach my Word, you feed my little ones. As you caress my babies, they grow into manhood. As you allow them to take their first steps of faith, you teach them to grow up and mature.

I see your needs. I see your desires for exploits. But as you surrender all to me, I will meet the deepest needs of your life. As you surrender my work to me, I will move through you in such a way that you will marvel at the move of my Spirit. I am Almighty God of strength, power and love. As you surrender your voice to me, you will flow with a fresh anointing, a fresh move of my Spirit, one you have longed for and desired. Reach up to me in praise. Reach out to others with my love. As you do, healing and deliverance will take place. Prison doors will open. I love you and I see your faithfulness. You will be rewarded.

> *The end of all things is near. Therefore be clear minded and self-controlled so that you can pray. Above all, love each other deeply because love covers over a multitude of sins.* I Peter 4:7-8

LOVE

DO THEY STILL WANT MILK

I see your circumstances and your condition and I am moved. I see your past needs and your future needs and I answer in due season, in due time. Hang on. Hang on. Hang on. The break-through is just about to come.

I know of your fasts, of your intercessions, of your prayers for your people, for the flock that I have entrusted to you. I know of your need for the flock to raise high above their circumstances and learn my Word, to cherish it, to hide it in their hearts. As a baby is often rebellious when told to do something for the first time, so they are like little babies, acting rebellious because they have been confronted with the truth of my Word. You have not lied to them. You have not told them an untruth. You have given them meat and they still want milk.

Not all are like them. Within the flock that I have entrusted you with is a nucleus of people who want to go on to the deeper things of me. Yes, feed them the deeper things of my Word. Feed the babies the milk and both will mature, both will grow and my kingdom will prosper.

Do not be discouraged for I have chosen you, I have called you to this work at this time. In the days ahead, before my return, I will be broadening you, expanding you to bring fresh and living water to many people, through the spoken word, through the sung word. I have seen your faithfulness against great odds and opposition. Yes, I have seen the persecution to you and your family. But remember, my son and my daughter, he who is faithful over little, I will put over much.

> *The Lord will guide you always; he will sat-*
> *isfy your needs in a sun-scorched land and will*
> *strengthen your frame. You will be like a well-wa-*
> *tered garden, like a spring whose waters never*
> *fail. Your people will rebuild the ancient ruins*
> *and will raise up the age-old foundations; you*
> *will be called Repairer of Broken Walls, Restorer*
> *of Streets with Dwellings.*   Isaiah 58:11-12

MATURITY

IS YOUR MINISTRY SMALL

There will come a day soon in which you will look back on these days when your flock was few in number and long for them again. As you grow, I will provide for each person the intimacy and love needed to meet the need of the hour and the day. Do not fear. I will bless this ministry. I will bring people in from various places. I will anoint my sheep with a spirit of evangelism. I have set this ministry apart to be a praise unto my name. This ministry is one of hope, of agape love, of miracles and evangelism. Be patient. Wait on me. I will move and answer your prayers.

He has made everything beautiful in its time. He has also set eternity in the hearts of men; yet they cannot fathom what God has done from beginning to end. I know that there is nothing better for men than to be happy and do good while they live. That everyone may eat and drink and find satisfaction in all his toil—this is the gift of God. I know that everything God does will endure forever; nothing can be added to it and nothing taken from it. God does it so that men will revere him.   Ecclesiastes 3:11-14

NUMBERS

ARE THERE OBSTACLES IN YOUR CHURCH

W eep no more my son. Cry no more my daughter. Surely as I parted the waters when Moses stretched forth his rod in faith, so I will do the same for you. Though the wall seems high, though the bricks seem many, yet my Spirit will remove each one, one by one, so that what was, is no more and what is, will come to pass. I the Lord remove obstacles. I the Lord increase strength. I the Lord part the deepest waters so you can walk on dry ground. As Moses my servant led a host of people to the other side, so you will do the same.

Already they are gathering. Already they are preparing in their heart, yes in their spirit, to move on ahead, to go forth into the promise land I have chosen for them. Yes, my Spirit is preparing even now and has been preparing for years to bring a people together during these last days who will glorify me. My timing is perfect.

I have seen your fasts, and they have been often. I have heard your intercessions and your prayers have gone directly to my Father's throne. I have seen your humble spirit, and I have seen you bent over, on your knees, prostrate upon the floor, or sitting in a chair praying. Every time you have breathed my name, I have breathed in the aroma of praise and I too have been filled. I too have been ministered to by you. I have seen you as you have strolled and lifted your hands toward heaven. All these things have not gone unnoticed and I am pleased with you.

I am working. I am working and a great breakthrough is imminent. People will come in and my promises will be fulfilled, for from a child I have been preparing you for this time. Even now my Spirit is preparing you for greater exploits and greater conquests in my name.

As I build your faith, I use it. As I challenge the spirit of man, faith grows and grows and grows till it becomes a full grown tree, full of luscious fruit, till it becomes the light for a whole city, till it becomes a drink of sweet wine for my body.

Be patient in all things. The wine vats are almost full and are ready to burst forth. Your greatest victories, greatest challenges of faith, greatest miracles are ahead, just around the corner. Be steadfast, unmovable and abound in my work. You will mount with the wings of eagles. You will run and not be weary. You will walk and not faint. You will jump in high places and you will know my Shekinah glory.

My Shekinah glory will descend upon your people, the young and the old alike. They too will know my presence so much so that they will not be able to stand. They will fall on their knees and cry, Jesus, Jesus, Jesus.

Be encouraged my son and my daughter. I do love you. Your work will be rewarded not only on earth, but in my Heavenly Kingdom as well. I am preparing you for leadership beyond your present understanding.

He has showed you, O man, what is good. And what does the Lord require of you? To act justly and to love mercy and to walk humbly with you ⌐ God.   Micah 6:8

OBSTACLES

ARE YOU ABOVE YOUR CONGREGATION

You ou know a lot about the lives of others, but instead of leaving the errors of their ways to my Holy Spirit to convict, you have tried to bring conviction by manipulation of words. You are going through a humbling process, a breaking, a time of repentance. As I show you things in the days ahead, you will be broken in contriteness before me, but afterwards will come the resurrection, a new man, a new life of anointed power. The breaking and molding will not be easy, but when I am finished, I will have a purified vessel. The fires are hot, but as each area is surrendered, purity will come forth.

I see your heart and the need for important feelings to be satisfied. As you humble yourself before me, a new quiet meekness will come forth with words of wisdom and knowledge, said in love so my body can identify with them. Some of your words are not being accepted, even though they are of me, because the people sense you are above them. As I move upon you, I will change all this and you will be exalted as you lay down your life before me.

I am moving upon you to be one with the body, one with the Lord, and one in the Spirit with the people. You will not be above them, nor beneath, but one. When this happens, a new mighty wave of my Spirit will take place in you, a fresh anointing of power, a fresh breeze. For the people will see Jesus and respond with waves of joy going throughout the whole congregation.

And whoever wants to be first must be your slave.
Just as the Son of Man did not come to be served,
but to serve, and to give his life as a ransom for
many.   Matthew 20:27-28

SERVANTHOOD

IS GOD SPEAKING CONCERNING HEALING

I say unto you my shepherd over my flock, you have been faithful to me against great obstacles and against great odds. I am pleased. You will rise with new hope, new vigor and new power, for the anointing of God shall come upon you, an anointing from the Father, an anointing of healing. You will rise with the power of my Spirit, for healing will flow through you and many in my flock will be set free.

Reach out my son with my anointing oil. Reach out in faith. A great wave of my Spirit will take place in your life. The desires that I have put within your heart will be fulfilled. You will grow, expand and reach out for my honor and for my glory. You will move out with anointed power. Your tent stakes shall be pulled up and expanded for my glory.

My hand is not shortened that it cannot save the vilest of sinners. My hand is not shortened that it cannot bring about revival fires. The fires of the old are being replaced by great flames of power. The flicker will be replaced by a great out-pouring of my Spirit. I am returning soon. I am coming for a bride that is ready. I am coming for a bride of honor and praise.

> *They went out and preached that people should repent. They drove out many demons and anointed many sick people with oil and healed them.* Mark 6:12-13

SPIRITUAL GIFTS

DO YOU DESIRE THE HOLY SPIRIT UPON
YOUR FLOCK

I move upon my servants in many ways and in different manners. I move on one with a word and another with great messages of hope, deliverance and healing. My anointing varies, but my anointing is consistent and strong on my servants who obey me with their whole heart. As I move in various ways and in different manners, so my glory varies in a church service. But as my people who are called by my name humble themselves and pray, my power and my glory descends, and the place comes alive with the fullness of my power and might. As my people praise my name, my glory descends, falls mighty, so much so that you cannot stand in my presence.

I know your hunger to be filled with my Spirit. I know your desire for my people. As you open your heart and mind for my presence to be manifested, it will be done. Nothing is impossible to those who believe, for my glory does rest upon you. My Spirit will move upon you, your family and upon the people I have placed you as shepherd over.

As my name goes forth in glory, my Spirit will descend and people will be healed. They will be set free. They will be set free. I am the God of all deliverance and all glory. My power will radiate from you and you will lay hands on the sick. They will recover. Miracles will be seen. People on sick beds will rise. As my name goes forth and breaks the bonds of wickedness, my glory will descend.

Be patient, steadfast, unmovable and abound in my work.
Walk in love. My flock will grow. A deluge of people will come
in. I am preparing you even now for the great task I have before
you. What you have desired will come to pass. Zion will be set
ablaze with my salvation.

I call. I prepare. I will raise up ministers out of you for my
glory. Give me praise. What you do not see is already accomplished in me. I am Jehovah Shammah. I am present with you.
I am present in this place.

*Arise, shine, for your light has come, and the
glory of the Lord rises upon you.* Isaiah 60:1

SPIRITUAL HUNGER

IS GOD MOVING TOO SLOW FOR YOU

Y ou are anxious about many things. As I parted the Red Sea for Moses, as I led the people over on dry ground, so I will do the same for you. I am moving. I am moving in the hearts of your people, and they will grow. They will grow to be people of maturity in the things of me. As I moved the Israelites through the many experiences of the wilderness, so I will move upon your people to mature them in the things of my Spirit.

I have seen your tears, dedication and fasts. I am pleased with a contrite heart, but the miracle is mine. I will move upon your people at the proper time and when my Spirit has gone before to prepare their hearts. A great breakthrough will come in your ministry. I will move upon the hearts of your people and they will burst forth in praise unto my name. As I filled the water pots with new wine, so I will fill your people with the new wine of my Spirit. As I filled the pots with oil till they overflowed in abundance and the widows' needs were met, so I will fill your pots full of oil till you flow abundantly with my resources.

Your voice is sanctified unto me. I have much ministry ahead for you. You will leave the shores of your dwelling place and go to new places in my name. Your ministry, yea mine, (for it is I the Lord who does great and mighty things through you) will overflow with glory unto my name. Souls will be saved. Souls will be baptized in my Spirit. Souls will be made whole in body and in spirit.

Do not weep. Do not fret. Do not withhold. I am broadening you for my honor and my glory. As I gave Gideon the victory with the mirrors of my power, so I will give you victory with the mirrors of my spirit and my blood. They reflect my glory and my image.

> *Though I walk in the midst of trouble, you pre-*
> *serve my life; you stretch out your hand against*
> *the anger of my foes, with your right hand you*
> *save me. The Lord will fulfill his purpose for*
> *me; your love, O Lord, endures forever—do not*
> *abandon the works of your hands.*Psalms 138:7-8

TIMING

IS GOD CALLING THE ELDERS TOGETHER

C all the elders together. Seek me at the appointed time and I will give you my plan, my direction, and my guidance for this my body and my church. It will not be a small plan, but a plan of vision and of an exploit. I will part all waters of unbelief as you seek me with all of your heart. Your men will flow with anointed power. Those that are crying out for my gifts to flow in manifestation will flow in power, in love and in strength. I have not appointed this body to be small in endeavors, but large in spirit and in vision. Have faith in me. Have faith in me.

Then the Lord replied: 'Write down the revelation and make it plain on tablets so that a herald may run with it. For the revelation awaits an appointed time; it speaks of the end and will not prove false. Though it linger, wait for it; it will certainly come and will not delay.'
Habakkuk 2:2-3

VISION

III. TO MY CHURCH

God's message to His people from the Book
of Genesis to Revelations is one of repentance,
redemption, holiness and love. It is an eternal
message to bring His creation into fellowship with
Him through the redemptive work of Jesus on the
cross of Calvary. *Salvation is found in no one else,
for there is no other name under heaven given to
men by which we must be saved.* (Acts 4:12)

The following messages are addressed to various states in
America and others to the Body of Christ in general. No matter
where we are living geographically, His people are joined by
the blood of Jesus and His desire for love and unity. God's truth
transcends time and location.

> *Therefore, as God's chosen people, holy and
> dearly loved, clothe yourselves with compassion,
> kindness, humility, gentleness and patience. Bear
> with each other and forgive whatever grievances
> you may have against one another. Forgive as the
> Lord forgave you. And over all these virtues put on
> love, which binds them all together in perfect unity.*

> *Let the peace of Christ rule in your hearts, since
> as members of one body you were called to
> peace. And be thankful. Let the word of Christ
> dwell in you richly as you teach and admonish*

one another with all wisdom, and as you sing psalms, hymns and spiritual songs with gratitude in your hearts to God. And whatever you do, whether in word or deed, do it all in the name of the Lord Jesus, giving thanks to God the Father through him. Colossians 3:12-17 (NIV)

TO THE CHURCH OF CALIFORNIA

I know of your deeds, of your ways and of your struggles. I know of your desire to serve me with all of your heart, with all fervor, with all honesty, and with all praise unto my name. Yes, my Spirit has been hovering, has been moving, and has been wooing many of you for years. Yes, my Spirit has been chastening and bringing into obedience many of you who have strayed from the truth. I Jesus love all of you with the love of my Father.

I have given myself to you on Calvary and now many of you are giving yourselves back to me. I am preparing to return soon. I am preparing my bride to be adorned with victory, with joy and with radiance.

I am calling out a people of praise unto my name, a people dedicated to serve at my feet, a people who will rise to victory and defeat the evil that is still present in this world. Yes, I have been preparing, since my ascension, to bring all things in subjection to me and to bring all my enemies under my feet.

Yes, my daughters and my sons, I am moving by my Spirit to bring together, before my return, a body of unity, power and beauty. I am not a God that divides, unless division comes for truth to prevail. I am not a God that brings schisms, unless schisms will bring about my will. Yes, I am a God that unifies all things by my purposes and plans. Can you suppose to ever understand my dealings completely? Can you ever suppose to understand me with human resources?

I am a Spirit and my dwellings are in the supernatural, are in the depths of no time and no space. I am a God of galaxy upon galaxy of knowledge and when that is conquered, there are a myriad and infinite number of more galaxies of knowledge. My purposes on earth are my purposes in the area of no time and no space.

Begin my children to speak by faith, love for one another. Do not divide over words, thoughts and misunderstandings. Quicken and hasten my return by unity and love for one another, a bride without spot or wrinkle.

My body is unique in California. My Church is to be strong here. I am calling many of you to rise with new power to go forth among the people who do not know me. You are to go with love and mercy. I am a God of infinite mercy upon the sinful, lost ways of men. Take up the cross and follow me. I have already been speaking to many of you to leave your present positions and enter my ministry.

You will know my leading in a new and vital way if you are obedient and walk by faith. What is money to me? Do I not own everything? I can give it to you in many different ways; through friends, through my body, by laying it on a side walk, by providing special talents and abilities to you like my servant Paul. My Angels can just drop it out of another realm to your feet at the right time and place as I provided food through my ravens to the prophet.

I need ministers, men, women and youth to enter full-time service for me. I am calling you out to salvation, deliverance and hope to a lost people. My time is short. My Spirit is moving quickly to do the greatest move that California has ever known. You will become like my early Church in which thousands were brought in a day to me. You will go from door to door. You will go into the restaurants, the bars, the ghetto, the tenements, and you will speak my name and people will be born again.

Listen for my Spirit. Do not leave your place of employment until I have prepared you and have told you so. There will be a witness of two or three and of my Word. Cling to my written Word for direction. You will know, that you know, that the potters hand is saying, "Now is the time." For some of you it will be today as confirmation of what I have already said to you. For others you need to be trained and schooled by my anointed leaders. Each person will be unique. Don't copy someone else's ministry. My Spirit moves in great variety.

Oh my Church in California, I brood over you like a mother hen and her chicks. I long to gather all of you and put you under my mighty wings to comfort and protect you. Listen to my anointed leaders. You will know their voice, for my sheep follow me.

Be open to my Holy Spirit. Do not fear Him, for He cannot be understood fully with your mind. Receive Him in authority and power. Let my Spirit take control of all areas of your life, to drive out what is not of me.

I have been calling many of you to support my ministries. Give of your resources to my work. I will bless you, bless you, and bless you. For some this will be easy, for you already have much. For others, this will be a step of faith. In either case, I will bless many times over.

Oh my church in California, do not walk in fear of what you hear. Not all of my children speak in hope and faith. If devastation comes, it will not touch your spirit if you are walking under my covering, in my covenant. It will not hurt you, it will not touch you, it will not move you. Does not my word say, "I never, never leave or forsake or let go."? Believe my Word; cling to it; walk in it; let it become a part of your daily life. Experiences and manifestations of my Spirit come and go, but my Word goes on forever.

Love one another. Love one another. Love one another. I will move in the churches in California in a way that has not preceded anything before or will ever come again. My warrior angels are already hovering over the State Capitol, over the leaders, over my leaders.

Pray! Pray! Pray! Gather yourselves together by two, by three, and by many. Pray and praise my name and what will come into existence is a mighty move of my Spirit.

CHURCH OF CALIFORNIA

TO THE CHURCH OF ILLINOIS

I know of your struggles. I know of your deeds. I know of your desire to be one; one in spirit, one in life, and one in purpose. I know of your deepest hurts and how you have struggled against great opposition to my Spirit. But, yes, my children, I am pleased with you, I am pleased, I am pleased.

All over Illinois I am calling out a glorious bride without spot or wrinkle. I am calling out a people who will worship me in Spirit and in truth. I am calling out men of authority in my Word. I am calling out men gifted with my Spirit who will take up the cross, leave the past behind and follow me unreservedly.

I am calling out women, gifted in my Spirit to move into areas and circles that have not been given my Word. I am calling out the young people and children to take a stand for me during these final days before my return.

Yes, time is quickly passing and soon time will be no more. We will all be one in the realm of no time and full eternity.

Bring souls in my children; bring them in my children before it is too late. My Spirit has prepared many to receive me as Savior and Lord. Give them the message of my saving power, my saving grace, and my saving sanctification.

Listen for my voice in all things. Be still, be silent, and listen for my leading and my word. Let my Spirit set you free to new mountain peaks of evangelism in my name. Look at the fields. Look and see the harvest ready to be gathered in.

Oh, my children, I love you, I love you, I love you. Be faithful in all things. Let my sweet Holy Spirit prompt you to greater exploits in my name. Nothing is impossible with me. I am a God of great patience with the children of men.

Pray! Pray! Pray! Pray them in, by one and twos and by many. No sin is too great in any that I bring across your path that it cannot be washed away and remembered no more. No problem is too heavy that I cannot set free and deliver out of.

Oh my people in the Church of Illinois, hear my still small voice. Hear my prompting voice. Hear my thunderous voice. I the Lord your God am getting ready to move in on the peoples of Illinois in a new and mighty way. Churches will multiply overnight. Churches will grow by leaps and bounds as people seek out the oasis in the midst of the desert. People are ready, my children. Bring them in from the highways and the byways. Talk about me when you sit at work, when you go to the store, wherever I shall lead. My Spirit will go before you in all things.

I am coming soon! I am coming soon! I am coming soon! Persecutions, difficulties, stresses and needs are nothing to me. I give abundant help, mercy and grace for all situations. I never leave. I never forsake. I never let go. Nothing shall separate us from one another. You are mine! Mine! Mine! Church of Illinois, you are mine to bring glory and honor to My Holy Name.

CHURCH OF ILLINOIS

TO THE CHURCH OF MAINE, CONNECTICUT & NEW HAMPSHIRE

Hear the voice of my Holy Spirit. Hear the voice of my sweet Jesus. Hear the voice of I AM. I, Jehovah Rophe, the God of all healing, deliverance, love and provision will meet with you this very hour. I Jehovah, the I AM of your fore-fathers, seek an audience with you.

My Spirit has been moving in a new and mighty way to bring you away from the shore, out of the past. My Spirit is doing a new and mighty thing across your state to bring people to the fresh, living waters of salvation and baptism. My Spirit has been moving to draw, to woo, to prompt into the depths of the written Word, to deeper theology, truths, hidden beneath the surface, like a sunken treasure chest, buried in the darkness of the waters. I have been calling many of you like disciples of old, to be fishers of men, to bring in the nets full of souls for my Kingdom. I am moving upon many of your hearts right now to answer the call.

Do not fear men and their abuse, for the abuse you take for suffering for my name is nothing to the torture they will receive if they do not come to me in faith believing. Take the ridicule as a good soldier of the cross. Does not a military man expect to receive artillery back when he fires his gun? Many of my lost children are acting under evil desires and evil prompting. Let my compassion and love rise in your souls and give the words of salvation with gentleness, prompted by my love in you. Do not be rude! Do not be rude! Do not be rude! My Spirit cannot work through arguments, only through love.

Rise up, oh young people with my Word. Do not sleep. But take the banner of love and the Sword of the Spirit to where I will lead you. Walk from door to door. Souls are already prepared behind them. Walk to the stores. Walk to places I will lead you to. Do not fear lest another walk ahead of you and steal what is mine. Walk for my Kingdom and no one else.

Rise up Oh Pastors, my shepherds, my anointed ones. Teach your people my Word. Teach! Teach! Teach! Heal the broken in heart through faith in Me and my Word, for I will not deny what I have spoken. I will not deny what my apostles through my Sprit have written. My Word is life to you and to your flock. Trust me, oh shepherds. Trust me and do not fear the ways of the Holy Spirit. They are not discernible to the natural mind and man's wisdom. But your reborn spirit speaks to you that He is true and right and moves in great mysterious ways. I am not understood with human concepts and thoughts. I Am that I AM, that I AM, a God of infinite wisdom, past finding out with the natural mind. Yes, I am moving all over the world and men, gifted with My Spirit are coming to new heights of evangelism, truth and manifestations of My Glory.

In a short time, children, it will not be strange for you to witness children getting up out of wheel chairs and walking for the first time in their life; for eyes to be open like my ministry of old; for deaf to hear, to speak, to shout, "Glory, Glory, Glory to the

Lamb of God that takes away the sins of the world, that is, that was, that forever more shall be." It will not be strange, different, or peculiar for I have and will be equipping all who are thirsty for the waters of life to flow through them. Signs and wonders, Pastors, will accompany your ministry, yes, my ministry, if my Word is taught in truth, and in entirety.

The coldness in your church will become a spark, then a blazing fire of power as you take a step of faith in my name and part the waters of unbelief. As I parted the Red Sea, so my Word going forth in anointed power breaks every yoke, every fetter, every bondage. I Am LIFE! I Am LIFE! I AM.

CHURCH OF MAINE, CONNECTICUT, & NEW HAMPSHIRE

TO THE CHURCH OF NEW YORK

Y our State is vast. Your State is great. Its power is like Babylon of old. Many people are crowding your streets and your places of transportation. Your churches' struggles are great. Your discouragements are many. Your faith is little in your eyes, but it is much in my eyes. Faith, even as small as a grain of mustard seed, supported with my Word, can accomplish great things for my Kingdom.

Do not look at the task before you and say it is too great. Was that my attitude, my feelings when my Son wept over the city of Jerusalem, over Israel? Yes, I sent into the world, the Redeemer of the whole earth, the whole atmosphere, the whole galaxy upon galaxy of planets and stars. No task is too great for you when my Spirit prompts and moves you. No job is too big and no sinner impossible to save.

Yes, my Spirit will draw them out from the deepest pits of despair, deepest dungeons of adultery, and deepest holes of sins darkest caves. Nothing, no nothing is impossible in My Name.

Look out of your windows my children. Look down the block. Look upon the streets. Do you not see the lost condition of souls? Many are like Mary Magdalene's wanting out of their situation, but no one is there to love and to help set free. What you see on the outside is nothing in my eyes. What I see are people ready to repent, ready to be let out to new homes, new dwellings for my honor and my glory.

Get up from your pews. Praise unto my name is an abomination to me if you are not fulfilling what I commissioned my disciples of old to do. Yes praise me, praise me, praise me. It will set you free. Take hold of that freedom and speak out the Good News of hope, deliverance, salvation and waters. Take my shield, take my life, and take my message to the lost. So many people are ready to repent all over New York. People will rise out of the gutters of life with a new song. Overnight they will be set free because when my Word is given in authority and in faith, life takes place. Visions are restored and people are delivered out of prisons.

Look my children. Look around you. Gather them into my barns of grain. I love you, and I am returning soon. The trumpet will blow that final call and up you will go to meet me in the air. My church shall be one. We shall be one.

Bring them in Pastors, leaders of my flock. Do not shrink back in fear and unbelief and say, "Oh, this one is beyond hope." No one is beyond my touch, my hand. Speak in love, in gentleness, in truth, in fullness of my Word to your people, yes my sheep. Lead them beside still waters. Lead them to green pastures. Hold their hand when they want to go back for fear of the beasts that lurk to devour them. Take my Authority over the areas of evil in your church and in your community. Speak my Words of faith from my Word and Satan's strongholds will be brought down under my feet to crush, to step on, and my return will come. I will come! I will come! I am coming back for my bride in splendor, majesty and power, saith the Lord.

CHURCH OF NEW YORK

TO THE CHURCH OF THE WEST

M any of you have great joy. Many of you have great abundance. Many of you are wealthy, wealthy. You are wealthy in this world's goods and wealthy in me. But, my children, I have this one thing against you. You grieve my Spirit. You grieve my Spirit. You grieve my Spirit.

My Holy Spirit has sought to bring many of you to deliverance in my Holy Name, but you have refused, you have refused, you have refused. Doctrine that takes my Spirit and puts Him in one moving and one moving alone, does not come from Me. My Spirit is like the wind. It is mighty. It is strong. It is soft and you cannot tell from where it comes or where it goes. My Spirit moves in various ways on different groups of people. Do not quench him by looking for one type of move by my Spirit.

Praise to Me from you has been like sweet incense before me. Praise to my name has been sweet to my nostrils. I know of your fullness. I know of your desires. I know how you long to be one with others. Let me set you free to be one in praise to me.

Praise me! Praise me! Praise me together and your weeping will turn to joy, your sorrows to laughter. You will be set free in all things and a great wave of my Spirit will pour upon you with my Shekinah Glory. People will be delivered, people set free, prison doors in churches all over the West open and you will grow, grow, grow. I am returning soon saith the Spirit of Grace.

CHURCH OF THE WEST

TO THE CHURCH OF WASHINGTON D.C.

The other day, for a day is like a thousand years to me, I looked down on you and saw how green everything was. Yes, I looked and saw the souls of men alive and vibrant for my truths. Yes, I looked and saw their willing spirit to follow me in all things. Yes, that was yesterday. That was another day and another time. But now my children, I see a new day. This is a day of indifference, a day of coldness, a day of lack of concern for the souls of men.

My children, I love you and my Spirit is willing to set you free from the past. My Spirit is willing and ready to do a new thing. My Spirit is able to deliver you now. My angels are hovering over churches, over the state capitol, over people. My angels are ready to minister to the needs of my children. They are moved by prayer, by my anointing and by My Word of command.

Yes, I am grieved. I am grieved, but I can and will do a new thing all over Washington. It will start by individuals, spread to the churches and then move upon the capitol. My anointed servants carry my authority and my power. I will prompt them and move them to do my will and they will respond.

All peoples of the earth look to Washington as they did to my leading with Israel of old. I am raising up prophets under my authority, to speak to the leadership in order to bring life to the world.

I am speaking to women to rise with my Word to bring it to those in places of power. I will give grace and mercy in abundance before judgment. I will give every chance, every opportunity to bring about change in my name. I am a God of patience and deliverance. Do not look at what you see. Do not take heed to what you read in newspapers and magazines. Weigh all against my word and you will be set free from fear.

Pray! Pray! Pray for those in authority, in the state capitol, in businesses, in churches and in homes. Do not give up and those in prison will walk out unharmed and untouched by the evil one.

Praise me! Praise me! Praise me! Let my blood and my Spirit be a unifying force, not menial doctrinal issues. Can anyone of you truly say that he knows all truth and teaching?

Gather yourselves together in small groups and in large numbers and sing praise unto my name and pray for one another that you may be healed. Do not look for manifestations of the supernatural, but look for love, love, love. This is the greatest of all my gifts. Love will blend and mend the deepest hurt, deepest woe and greatest problem. Let love rule in your hearts from within, from your homes, your churches, you businesses and the state capitol.

A word now to the President: Seek my face early, before all others in your household are up. I will speak to you in a word, in a whisper, and through my written word. Your deepest needs for decisions will be met and as I gave authority to my kings of old, even King Sennacarib, I will give the same to you. Solomon had wisdom because He asked for it. Continue to ask and you will receive. I will guide you and I will direct you. I will surround you with My council and my direction.

CHURCH OF WASHINGTON D.C.

I WILL CHASTEN

As I destroyed the Edomites, so I will chasten those in my body who look with glee upon the destruction of another brother. As I chastened those of my body who have gone out from under my canopy into wolves' territory, so I will chasten those who speak words of faith, yet walk in self-righteousness toward their brothers and sisters who do not believe. Obadiah, my servant, spoke words to Edom of coming devastation because they thought they could not be brought down from their lofty position. So those in my body who are lofty in faith believing, yet are not concerned nor weep over their brothers and sisters, who do not believe the same way, will be brought down too.

Weep my children over those who do not believe. Lament and mourn over their condition. Do not let your pride hinder my Spirit's moving in the life of others.

My Spirit works through love and love alone. Love your brother. Love your sister and pray. Let your words be in patience and kindness. Wasn't I patient with you till you came to the truth!

> *You should not look down on your brother in the day of his misfortune, nor rejoice over the people of Judah in the day of their destruction, nor boast so much in the day of their trouble.Obadiah 1:12*

CHASTEN

I SEEK CHILDLIKENESS

There are those in my body who are whirling and whirling and not taking time to pause at my feet.

There are those who are in the Spirit, but Satan is seeking to distract them from my move to go down a wrong path. If your eyes turn from my Spirit's leading, there will be a great fall.

There are those, like little children on a playground, who whirl and whirl till they fall down. It is such childlikeness that I seek among my people so my Spirit can move freely. It is such childlikeness that I search for that will allow my Spirit to move unhindered. It is such childlikeness that I seek from my people to trust me as a loving heavenly Father. Even when failure comes, such childlike trust in me will cause strength and maturity to grow.

> *Therefore, whoever humbles himself like this child is the greatest in the kingdom of heaven.*
> Matthew 18:4

CHILDLIKE

IS YOUR BODY HOLY

There are many of you whose lives are going around too fast. You keep moving and moving and moving, not stopping to listen to my word. I am calling forth my people to pause, to reflect, to slow down, and to hear my still small voice of love. If you continue in the direction and motion you are going, you will fall, and you will come crashing down. I am calling forth my body to consecration, prayer, and giving of ones total body for my purposes and plans.

Listen for my voice in all things. I am building a church, a temple consecrated unto me. Let me cleanse what is not of me. Submit to me in all things and let my Spirit set you free to soar to the heights with wide spread wings. My temple shall not be profaned but holy, dedicated unto me for my plans and purposes to be accomplished.

Give of your best to my work. Let my kingdom be built. As my kingdom is built, glory goes up to my Father and my glory then shines upon you. Dig deep into the wells of my Spirit. Allow my springs of living water to flow from your life and you will be set free.

> *Do you not know that your body is a temple of the Holy Spirit, who is in you, whom you have received from God? You are not your own; you were bought at a price. Therefore honor God with your body.* I Corinthians 6:19-20

HOLINESS

YOUR PRAISE DELIGHTS ME

Your praise has been a delight to me. I would desire that all of my children would praise me with their whole heart, soul and mind. As my Spirit is moving over the face of the earth, a great wave of praise and joy will take place. Churches all over the world will rise to a new depth of understanding in me. People will mount with the joy bells of praise, love and intercession for one another. I am moving swiftly and I am coming back for a glorious bride of radiance and beauty in me.

He who sacrifices thank offerings honors me,
and he prepares the way so that I may show him
the salvation of God.   Psalm 50:23

PRAISE

I WILL VINDICATE MY BODY

I am the Lord your God that visits the children of men. I am the Lord your God that gives strength. I am the Lord your God that walks before and brings help, brings vindication, brings justice. I can do all these things.

I will go before my body and vindicate what Satan has sought to tear down. I will go before my body and bring justice and happiness to its ailing parts, for many of my children have been degraded because of Satan's tactics. I will lift up my name before the presence of my enemies and they shall fall and weep and mourn for a day of visitation is coming, a day of hope and power, a day of courage and strength. So do not weep my children and do not mourn. I see the devices of man and they are nothing in my sight.

I am raising up warriors, mighty like David's army of old, who are fit for battle. The enemy shall flee with the power of my Word going forth like lightening into the dark corners of the world. So do not grieve, but look up, my children. Your redemption draws nigh.

> *The Lord will march out like a mighty man, like a warrior he will stir up his zeal; with a shout he will raise the battle cry, and will triumph over his enemies.* Isaiah 42:13

VINDICATION

WORK WHILE IT IS DAY

My Spirit will not always chide with men. My Spirit will not always woo to cleansing and forgiveness in me. The days are coming upon the earth when my Spirit will be lifted and work will be no more.

Work while it is day, my children. The night comes soon when no man can work. Look unto those fields. They are like ripe, luscious grapes ready to be picked. They are like full grown corn ready to be plucked.

Work while you can, while my Spirit is moving. Do not say in your heart that the task is too difficult, that the task is too hard. Is anything too hard for me to do? Is anything too difficult for me? Is anything too difficult for my Spirit to handle? I am a mighty God, a mighty warrior, a mighty lover, a mighty strengthener, and a mighty deliverer. Have faith in me, in my power and nothing shall be impossible unto you.

I am moving all over the world and my Spirit is drawing out a purified body who will worship me in Spirit and in truth. Work! Be diligent for my life to be manifested in you. Then I can draw all men unto me for they will see Jesus.

> *As long as it is day, we must do the work of him*
> *who sent me. Night is coming, when no one can*
> *work.*   John 9:4

WORK

CPSIA information can be obtained at www.ICGtesting.com
Printed in the USA
LVOW11s0349171115

462925LV00001B/27/P